W9-AVL-781

New Jersey v. T.L.O.

Drug Searches in Schools

Deborah A. Persico

Landmark Supreme Court Cases

Enslow Publishers, Inc.

44 Fadem Road	PO Box 38
Box 699	Aldershot
Springfield, NJ 07081	Hants GU12 6BP
USA	UK

This book is dedicated to my husband and best friend, Joseph.

Library of Congress Cataloging-in-Publication Data

Persico, Deborah A.
    New Jersey v. T. L. O.: drug searches in schools / Deborah A. Persico.
      p. cm. — (Landmark Supreme Court cases)
    Includes bibliographical references and index.
    Summary: Details the Supreme Court case that dealt with drug searches by public
school employees and debated the Fourth Amendment rights of students.
    ISBN 0-89490-969-X
    1. New Jersey—Trials, litigation, etc.—Juvenile literature. 2. Trials (Narcotic laws)—
New Jersey—Juvenile literature. 3. Searches and seizures—United States—Juvenile
literature. [1. New Jersey—Trials, litigation, etc. 2. Trials (Narcotic laws) 3. Searches
and seizures.] I. Title II. Series.
KF224.N38P47   1998
345.73'0277—dc21   97-38667
                                         CIP
                                         AC

Printed in the United States of America

10 9 8 7 6 5 4 3 2

Photo Credits: Library of Congress, pp. 27, 69, 75, 80, 84, 92, 104; Maureen
Urban, p. 62; Middlesex County Prosecutor's Office, p. 46; National Archives, pp.
14, 25; Nhu-Mai Simon, p. 9; *The Star Ledger*, p. 43, 90, 99.

Cover Photo: Joseph Virgilio

Contents

Acknowledgments

The author would like to offer special thanks to the following people:

Lois DeJulio, Esq., for her gracious assistance and personal insight.

Frederick A. Simon, Esq., for his assistance with the initial proceedings in T.L.O.'s case.

Kenneth Lebrato, Esq., for his insight into how the *T.L.O.* case began.

Ralph and Lena Persico, for their loving support.

Joseph Virgilio, Esq., my husband and best friend, for his help and support in preparing this manuscript.

Dorothy Flaherty, my friend, for her insight and guidance.

1

The Search of T.L.O.'s Purse

During school hours on March 7, 1980, in Piscataway, New Jersey, high school math teacher Lenore Chen walked into the girls' bathroom. There she saw two girls holding what she thought to be lit cigarettes. One of the girls was a fourteen-year-old ninth grader whose initials were T.L.O. Smoking was permitted in certain designated areas in the school. Regulations did not permit smoking in the bathrooms, however. Ms. Chen escorted T.L.O. and the other girl to the principal's office. Here she told Assistant Vice Principal Theodore Choplick what she had seen.

Mr. Choplick asked the girls if they had been smoking in the bathroom. The girl who was with T.L.O.

admitted she had been smoking. Mr. Choplick assigned her to a three-day smoking clinic. T.L.O., on the other hand, answered not only that she had not been smoking, but that she did not smoke at all. Based on what Ms. Chen had told him, Mr. Choplick decided to investigate further. He directed T.L.O. to his private office. He closed the door and T.L.O. sat down in a chair in front of his desk. Mr. Choplick sat down at his desk and then demanded that T.L.O. give him her purse. She complied.

When Mr. Choplick opened T.L.O.'s purse he saw a pack of cigarettes in plain view. He picked up the package, held it up, and said to T.L.O., "You lied to me."[1] As Mr. Choplick removed the cigarettes, he also saw a package of rolling papers for cigarettes. When he confronted T.L.O. with the rolling papers, she denied they belonged to her.

Mr. Choplick's experience in school had taught him that rolling papers were a sign that a person might smoke marijuana. With this in mind, he continued looking through T.L.O.'s purse. He found a metal smoking pipe, one plastic bag of what he believed to be marijuana, and a wallet containing forty dollars in one-dollar bills. Inside a separate compartment of the purse he found two letters and an index card. The index card read "People who owe me money." It was followed by a list of names and amounts of $1.50 and $1.00. Mr. Choplick read the letters, one from T.L.O. to another student and a return letter. They indicated to him that T.L.O. was selling drugs.

Police Called In

Mr. Choplick first called T.L.O.'s mother. Then he called the police. T.L.O.'s mother agreed to take T.L.O. to the police station for questioning. At police headquarters, an officer advised T.L.O. of her rights under the landmark Supreme Court case *Miranda* v. *Arizona*. She had a right to remain silent and not answer any questions; she had a right to an attorney; and anything she said to the police could be used against her at a trial.[2] T.L.O. signed a document stating that she would answer questions without an attorney present.

In her mother's presence, T.L.O. admitted to the police that all of the items Mr. Choplick found inside her purse belonged to her. She also admitted that she had been selling marijuana in school for one dollar per "joint," or marijuana cigarette. She also said that she had sold between eighteen and twenty joints at school that morning. Based on T.L.O.'s confession and the evidence Mr. Choplick had seized from her purse, the state of New Jersey filed a formal complaint against her in the juvenile and domestic relations court of Middlesex County. The complaint charged her with possession of marijuana with the intent to distribute. The complaint used only T.L.O.'s initials, not her full name. In juvenile cases, state law requires that the name of the juvenile remain confidential.

T.L.O. Suspended From School

T.L.O.'s problems with the criminal court system caused her additional problems with her school record. The Piscataway Board of Education learned of the incident, the evidence Mr. Choplick found, and the complaint filed against T.L.O. It then suspended T.L.O. from school for three days for smoking in the bathroom. It suspended her for another seven days for possession of drugs on school property. T.L.O.'s parents hired attorney Frederick A. Simon of the New Jersey law firm of Rosenberg & Simon to represent their daughter.

What would happen at T.L.O.'s trial? How would the decision affect her school record? Would the marijuana, pipe, money, letters, and index card that Mr. Choplick found inside T.L.O.'s purse be used as evidence against her? Would it matter that Mr. Choplick did not have a search warrant that authorized him to look inside T.L.O.'s purse?

After their daughter was charged with possession of marijuana, T.L.O.'s parents hired attorney Frederick A. Simon, shown here, to represent their daughter in court.

The United States Supreme Court would eventually become interested in T.L.O.'s case—but why? How would the Supreme Court's decision affect the rights of students and school officials in public schools around the country? In order to answer these questions, let us step back in history to see how the issues raised in T.L.O.'s case developed.

2

The History of Search and Seizure Law

The original thirteen colonies expressed anger toward Great Britain's domination years before the American Revolution (1775–1783). In 1772 Samuel Adams helped compile the "Rights of the Colonists and a List of Infringements and Violations of Rights."[1] In it he voiced the concern of many future revolutionaries. He denounced Great Britain's use of the general warrant. This was a document that allowed British officers to break down the door of a person's home and seize any goods they thought were evidence of a crime. Adams wrote:

> Thus, our houses and even our bedchambers are exposed to be ransacked, our boxes chests and trunks broke open ravaged and plundered by wretches whom no prudent man would venture to employ even as

menial servants. . . . Those Officers may under colour
of law and the cloak of a general warrant break thro'
the sacred rights of the Domicil, ransack men's houses
. . . and with little danger to themselves commit the
most horred [sic] murders.[2]

Developing the Bill of Rights

It was this anger that led the colonies in 1776 to declare
the general warrant illegal. The Virginia Declaration of
Rights was adopted on June 12, 1776. It was followed
by similar declarations in Maryland, Pennsylvania,
North Carolina, and Massachusetts. The declarations
made it clear that the colonists would not tolerate
general warrants any longer.

This philosophy surfaced again in 1787 when the
newly formed federation of the United States, free of
British rule, drafted its own Constitution. The document was submitted for approval by the states and was
officially declared in effect in 1789. It did not include
the Bill of Rights, however. Virginian James Madison
was a member of the new House of Representatives. He
looked to the individual state constitutions for guidance
in developing a bill of rights. He wanted to include a
provision about search and arrest warrants. The propos-
al Madison submitted is almost identical to the
following words, which we now know as the Fourth
Amendment to the Constitution of the United States:

The right of the people to be secure in their persons, houses, papers, and effects, against unreasonable searches and seizures, shall not be violated, and no Warrants shall issue, but upon probable cause, supported by Oath or affirmation, and particularly describing the place to be searched, and the persons or things to be seized.[3]

Fourth Amendment Guarantees

The amendment clearly guaranteed privacy and security to all citizens. The specific language used in the amendment, however, would lend itself to a multitude of interpretations for many years to come. What is a search and seizure? What is an unreasonable search and seizure? What did the drafters mean by the term "probable cause"? When does a person have a legitimate expectation of privacy in his or her property? Who is subject to the restrictions of the Fourth Amendment? What is the remedy for a violation of the Fourth Amendment?

What Is Search and Seizure?

In 1886 the United States Supreme Court had an opportunity to answer the first question—what is a search and seizure? In *Boyd* v. *United States* the federal government argued that a court order requiring the defendant to turn over his private accounting books, invoices, and records did not amount to a search and

James Madison was largely responsible for the inclusion of the Fourth Amendment in the United States Constitution. He believed that citizens had a right against unjust searches and seizures by government officials.

seizure under the Fourth Amendment. Search and seizure did not occur, the government argued, because the federal agents did not forcibly enter the defendant's home to search for his papers. The Supreme Court did not agree that the Fourth Amendment is triggered only where there is forcible entry. It held that the court order amounted to a search and seizure. It also held that an order requiring a person to turn over evidence that may be incriminating, violates that defendant's Fifth Amendment privilege against self-incrimination.[4] Twenty-eight years after *Boyd*, in 1914, the Supreme Court continued to develop its interpretation of the Fourth Amendment. It heard arguments in the case of *Weeks* v. *United States*.[5] A federal marshal had entered the home of Fremont Weeks without a search warrant and confiscated his personal papers. The trial court had allowed the prosecutor, the attorney for the government, to use that evidence against Weeks. He was convicted of a federal offense. Fremont Weeks appealed his case all the way to the Supreme Court.

Cases at the State Level

The long road Fremont Weeks traveled to the Supreme Court in 1914 is basically the same road criminal defendants must travel today. Generally, if a defendant believes evidence has been seized in violation of Fourth

Amendment rights, a document known as a motion to suppress evidence is filed with the trial court. If the trial court allows the government to use that evidence at trial and the defendant is convicted, found guilty of the crime, the defendant can ask a higher court, usually called a court of appeals, to review the case. If the court of appeals agrees with the defendant, it will reverse the conviction. That means it will strike the defendant's conviction from the record. It will also order the trial court to conduct a new trial without allowing the use of the improperly seized evidence. In most instances, because of the crucial nature of most evidence, a prosecutor will then dismiss the case. This usually occurs because there is not enough evidence to support a conviction.

If the court of appeals disagrees with the defendant in a state case, the defendant can appeal to a state court of last resort. This is usually called a state supreme court. If that court upholds the conviction, the defendant may then appeal directly to the United States Supreme Court.

Cases at the Federal Level

On the other hand, if the defendant was convicted in a federal district court, the trial court level of the United States court system, an appeal is made first to a federal circuit court of appeals. Then an appeal can be made directly to the United States Supreme Court.

Fremont Weeks's case started in a federal district court and ended in the United States Supreme Court. The Supreme Court agreed with Weeks. It ruled that because federal agents searched Weeks's home without a warrant, the search was clearly unreasonable under the Fourth Amendment. Because of this, the evidence should have been suppressed. To suppress evidence means that the court excludes its use at trial. Suppressing evidence in this way is commonly known as making use of the exclusionary rule. Did the *Weeks* decision mean that law enforcement officers would *always* need a warrant before they could search? The answer, as you will see, is no.

Probable Cause and Searches

Courts generally begin with the theory that any search or seizure of evidence that violates a person's personal security is per se, in and of itself, unreasonable. This is true unless a court issues a warrant based on probable cause.[6] Not surprising, there are many exceptions to the general rule. The first exception is that in some circumstances the law enforcement officer can justify a warrantless search if there is probable cause for the search.

What did the drafters of the Fourth Amendment mean by probable cause? In 1925 the United States Supreme Court defined probable cause in a case that would be cited by T.L.O. almost sixty years later. In *Carroll* v. *United States* the Supreme Court found that probable cause exists if a police officer has trustworthy information showing that a crime has occurred and that evidence of that crime will be found in a certain place. Under these circumstances the judge will issue a legal document, called a warrant. This document authorizes the officer to search for and seize the items named in the warrant and to arrest the person named in the warrant.[7]

The *Carroll* Court carved out one of the first major exceptions to the warrant requirement, using the term "probable cause." For search and seizure of evidence, the Court noted a difference between evidence concealed in a house or similar place, and evidence being transported in a moving vehicle such as a car, boat, or airplane. Because a vehicle can be quickly moved before a warrant can be issued, the *Carroll* Court held that a law enforcement officer may legally search a vehicle without a warrant. This can be done if there is probable cause to believe a crime has occurred and that the evidence is in the vehicle. Did the *Carroll* case mean that a police officer must always have probable cause whenever a search is conducted without a warrant? Again, the answer is no.

Warrantless Searches

The Supreme Court created exceptions to the warrant requirement. It also determined that in some cases government agents could justify a warrantless search even if they did not have probable cause. In the landmark case of *Terry* v. *Ohio* in 1968, the Justices were called upon to determine whether Mr. Terry's Fourth Amendment rights had been violated. A police officer patted down Terry's overcoat, felt a pistol in the inside pocket, tried to remove it but was unable to, and then removed Terry's coat and the pistol—all without a warrant.[8]

The Supreme Court consists of nine Justices. It uses a democratic system to decide cases. In other words, the majority rules. In *Terry*, the majority of the Justices agreed that Terry had been seized by the police officer and subjected to a search within the "reasonableness" standard of the Fourth Amendment. But did that mean the officer should have had a warrant and probable cause to search?

The officer, Cleveland Police Detective Martin McFadden, had testified in the trial court. He had reason to believe that Terry and two others were planning to rob a store. He saw Terry and another man standing together on a street corner for a long time. He watched as they paced along the same route, pausing to stare in the same store window. He then saw them join a third man. Detective McFadden decided to investigate.

Detective McFadden did not have probable cause to believe that Terry had actually committed a crime. Chief Justice Earl Warren recognized, though, that it would have been poor police work for the detective not to investigate. Warren further wrote on behalf of the Court that it would be unreasonable to deny police the power to protect themselves from potentially armed and dangerous suspects under these circumstances. Consequently, the Court ruled that police are justified in conducting a search for weapons for their own protection. They can do this where they have reasonable grounds to believe that "criminal activity may be afoot." They can also do this when the people with whom they are dealing may be armed and dangerous.[9]

The Supreme Court had ruled that police officers do not always need probable cause to justify a search or seizure. It then extended the *Terry* v. *Ohio* "reasonableness" standard to many other types of searches and seizures. For example, police may search a passenger compartment of a car if they have reasonable suspicion of criminal activity.[10] The United States Border Patrol is authorized to stop a vehicle and question its occupants. This can be done if the agents have reasonable suspicion that the vehicle may contain illegal aliens.

In some instances, the Supreme Court has recognized a need for states to regulate certain activities for the good of the general public. In these cases, the Court has authorized searches and seizures without a warrant, probable cause, *or* reasonable suspicion. Government agents can inspect mines and the businesses of gun dealers and alcohol dealers. The Coast Guard or Customs Service can board a vessel and examine documents. Fire fighters can remain in a building to investigate the cause of a fire after it has been extinguished. Why would the Supreme Court allow so many exceptions? Doesn't the Fourth Amendment *require* both a warrant and probable cause?

Let's take another look at the language of the Fourth Amendment—"The right of the people to be secure . . . against unreasonable searches and seizures. . . ." The Supreme Court has emphasized time and again that the Constitution does not forbid *all* searches and seizures—it forbids only *unreasonable* searches and seizures. The Court has determined that in many instances, searches and seizures are *reasonable* even though government agents did not have a warrant *or* probable cause to believe a crime had been committed.

The Balancing Test

If some searches and seizures require probable cause and some do not, how does the Supreme Court make that determination? Generally, it uses a balancing test. It considers the privacy interests of the individual searched, as well as the reasons the government wants to search. An individual must first show a reasonable "expectation of privacy" in the property searched. For example, placing an object in a container like a purse or suitcase that protects it from view demonstrates an expectation of privacy. The government must show the reasons for the search—for example, the health, welfare, or safety of the general public—are more important than the individual's privacy.

The "balancing test" courts use depends, for the most part, on the particular categories of searches. For example, in car searches the courts balance a car owner's right to privacy against the government's interest in securing evidence that could be moved very easily. In searches by health officials, courts balance a business owner's right to privacy against the likelihood that serious public health risks could go undetected. Fourth Amendment issues can be raised in a variety of situations in federal and state courts alike. That was not always the case.

Fourth Amendment Applying
Only to Federal Cases

In very early cases the United States Supreme Court held that the Fourth Amendment applied only to federal cases.[11] Federal crimes include espionage (spying), income tax evasion, destruction of national defense materials, violation of immigration laws, and possession and sale of drugs. The laws of the United States are enforced by United States attorneys in federal courts.

Due Process and the Fourteenth Amendment

In 1949, in the case of *Wolf* v. *Colorado*, the Supreme Court took a step that would affect thousands of cases to come.[12] It began by discussing the Fourteenth Amendment to the Constitution, adopted in 1868. This amendment prohibits any state from depriving any person "of life, liberty, or property, without due process of law. . . ."[13] This is known as the Due Process Clause of the Fourteenth Amendment. Due process means that before the state can take away a person's life, freedom, or property, that person is entitled to a fair hearing. The hearing also must follow certain rules of procedure. In a monumental step, the *Wolf* Court ruled that the concept of liberty in the Fourteenth Amendment includes the right of privacy contained in the Fourth Amendment.

Justice Felix Frankfurter wrote the opinion in *Wolf*. The Fourteenth Amendment did not specifically mention searches and seizures. Frankfurter reasoned, however, that the Fourteenth Amendment incorporated the rights of the Fourth Amendment. Therefore, states were required, from that time forward, to follow the restrictions of the Fourth Amendment when enforcing their own laws. State criminal laws include possession of illegal drugs, armed robbery, assault, and murder. State laws are enforced by prosecutors (also called district attorneys or state attorneys) in state courts.

Fourth Amendment Now Applying to State Cases

After the *Wolf* case, the Fourth Amendment applied to state cases. The exclusionary rule, however, still did not apply to state cases. That meant that if a state, county, or city police officer seized evidence illegally, the evidence was still admissible against defendants in most state courts. Then, in 1961, in the landmark decision *Mapp* v. *Ohio*, the Supreme Court extended the exclusionary rule. It would now apply to state cases.[14] From that day forward, all evidence illegally seized by police, for either a federal or state case, could no longer be used as evidence against a defendant.

In all of the Fourth Amendment cases discussed so

Justice Felix Frankfurter delivered the Supreme Court's opinion in *Wolf v. Colorado*, which declared that states had to follow the restrictions of the Fourth Amendment just as the federal government did.

far, convicted defendants asked the Supreme Court to review the conduct of law enforcement officers and other government agents. The Supreme Court had ruled long ago that the Fourth Amendment did not apply to searches conducted by private citizens. But are law enforcement officers and other government agents the only ones who are subject to the limitations of the Fourth Amendment? What about public school officials? Are they government agents because they are employed by the state government? Does the Fourth Amendment apply to them? These questions would not be completely answered until T.L.O.'s case reached the United States Supreme Court. In the meantime the state and federal courts struggled with possible answers—and they did not always agree.

Who Is Subject to the Fourth Amendment?

On one side were courts in the states of Alaska, California, and Texas. They held that public school officials are not subject to the constraints of the Fourth Amendment.[15] Those courts supported the idea that public school officials are not government agents. Instead, they are private parties who act *in loco parentis*—a Latin phrase meaning "in the place of a parent."[16] The principle of *in loco parentis*, more than two hundred years old, was explained in 1769:

In 1961, these members of the Supreme Court heard the case of *Mapp* v. *Ohio*, regarding whether illegally seized evidence could be used in state cases. After hearing the case, the Court ruled that the exclusionary rule applied to state cases just as it applied to those of the federal government.

[The father] may also delegate part of his parental authority, during his life, to the tutor or schoolmaster, of his child; who is then *in loco parentis*, and has such a portion of the power of the parent committed to his charge, *viz* that of restraint and correction, as may be necessary to answer the purposes for which he is employed.[17]

The Fourth Amendment in Schools

Courts that followed the doctrine of *in loco parentis* held that parents entrust their children to the care of the schools. Therefore, the schools were responsible not only for educating the children, but also for protecting them while they were in the school's custody. Using the doctrine of *in loco parentis*, the courts in Alaska, California, and Texas held that teachers, like parents, should be left free to discipline their students and maintain order in the schools. The *in loco parentis* doctrine basically assumes that students have no legitimate expectation of privacy in their personal property, such as purses, gym bags, or clothing. Parents have authority to search their child's property at will and are not subject to the restrictions of the Fourth Amendment. Because of this, some courts held that school officials are not subject to the Fourth Amendment either.

On the other side of the argument, other courts recognized that students do have a legitimate expectation of privacy in their personal belongings. For example, students need to bring to school certain items such as keys, money, and school supplies. They may also carry purses, wallets, or bags that contain personal items like photographs or diaries. Does that mean that students give up all rights to privacy just because they bring the items onto school property? Many courts said no.

If students have an expectation of privacy in their personal property, where does that leave school officials and the Fourth Amendment? According to many courts, it meant that schools are subject to the Fourth Amendment. Now came the more difficult question— What standard would apply to school officials who conducted searches of a student's personal property? Would it be probable cause or a lesser standard?

One court in Louisiana held that the Fourth Amendment applies to searches by public school officials. It also found, however, that any search of student property conducted by a school official who does not have probable cause is unreasonable under the Fourth Amendment.[18]

The majority of the courts though, reached a middle ground. New York, Delaware, Florida, Illinois, Michigan, New Mexico, Washington, Wisconsin, and several federal courts held that the Fourth Amendment applies to searches conducted by public school authorities.[19] But they also held that because of the special needs of the school environment—to train, educate, and maintain discipline—school officials do not need probable cause to search. These courts recognized the increasingly serious problems of drug use and violent crimes in schools. Searches would be upheld in the following circumstance: if the school official had a reasonable suspicion that the search would uncover evidence of a violation of either school disciplinary rules, or a state or federal law.

Various states were deciding on their own whether the Fourth Amendment applied to public school searches and which standard—probable cause or reasonable suspicion—would justify searches. Meanwhile the United States Supreme Court was also paving the way for T.L.O.'s case. It had not yet ruled on the specific issue that T.L.O. would eventually present. It was, however, analyzing the relationship between the Constitution and public schools in other areas.

The First Amendment in Schools

In 1943 the Court examined how the First Amendment, which guarantees all citizens the right to religious freedom, affected a West Virginia board of education's regulation. It required that all teachers and students in public schools salute the American flag.[20] In

Board of Education v. *Barnette*, children belonging to Jehovah's Witnesses, a religious organization, had been expelled from school for refusing to salute the flag. Their religion did not allow this type of ceremony. School officials threatened to send the children to schools for juvenile delinquents. The state of West Virginia brought criminal charges against the parents for causing the delinquency.

The majority of the Justices on the Supreme Court found that the First Amendment did not allow the state to force students to salute the flag. They believed that the First Amendment's right of freedom of religion was so important that a state could not limit it by state-enacted regulations.

Twenty-five years later, in 1968, four Iowa public schoolchildren from the Tinker family—John, fifteen years old; Mary Beth, thirteen years old; Hope, eleven years old; and Paul, eight years old—were suspended from school for wearing black armbands. This was their way of protesting the Vietnam War. In *Tinker* v. *Des Moines School District*, the Supreme Court was again asked to review a case where students' exercise of their First Amendment rights collided with school rules.[21] This time the First Amendment right involved freedom of speech.

In powerful language that would later be cited in *T.L.O.*, Justice Abe Fortas wrote the opinion for the

Supreme Court. In it, he made it clear that students do not shed their constitutional rights once they enter a school. He wrote:

> School officials do not possess absolute authority over their students. Students in school as well as out of school are "persons" under our Constitution. They are possessed of fundamental rights which the State must respect, just as they themselves must respect their obligations to the State.[22]

He also made it clear, however, that if a student disrupts the class or is disorderly, that conduct is not protected by the Constitution.[23]

In the *Tinker* case there was no evidence that any classes were interrupted. Nor were there any threats or acts of violence on school property as a result of the students wearing black armbands. The Court concluded that "our Constitution does not permit officials of the State to deny their form of expression."[24]

Justice Hugo L. Black had agreed with the majority opinion in the *Barnette* case. He strenuously objected, however, to the Court's opinion in *Tinker*. His written dissent brought out some of the intense battles that would arise over T.L.O.'s case. According to Justice Black, the Supreme Court had never held that students have constitutional rights to freedom of speech or expression in school. Public school students, Justice Black wrote, are not "sent to the schools at public expense to broadcast political or any other views to educate and inform the public."[25] Rather, public schools are operated "to give students an opportunity to learn, not to talk politics by actual speech, or by 'symbolic' speech."[26]

Justice Black warned that students would "soon believe it is their right to control the schools rather than the right of the States. . . ." He wrote, "I, for one am not fully persuaded that school pupils are wise enough, even with this Court's expert help from Washington, to run the . . . public school systems in our 50 States."[27]

Students' Rights vs. Schools' Rights

The Supreme Court continued to address the collision of student and school rights involving other constitutional amendments. In *Goss* v. *Lopez*, Ohio public high school students were suspended from school for misconduct.[28] The school did not give them a chance to defend their actions at a hearing before suspending them. The students appealed their suspensions. They argued that the Due Process Clause of the Fourteenth Amendment required that they be notified in advance of their suspension. It also allowed an opportunity for a hearing before they could be suspended. The Supreme Court agreed.

Under Ohio law the students had a legitimate claim

for the right to a public education. Ohio had chosen to extend the right to an education to its residents even though it was not obligated to do so. As such, the Supreme Court ruled that the Fourteenth Amendment required due process, or notice and a hearing, before the state could deprive a student of the right to attend school.

If the First and Fourteenth Amendments applied to public schools, did that mean that all constitutional amendments applied? In 1977 the Supreme Court heard the case of *Ingraham* v. *Wright.*[29] In the 1970s corporal (physical) punishment was permitted in public schools in every state except Massachusetts and New Jersey. James Ingraham and Roosevelt Andrews were both students at the Charles R. Drew Junior High School in Dade County, Florida. They asked the Supreme Court to find that paddling a public school student constituted cruel and unusual punishment. The boys felt it was in violation of the Eighth Amendment to the Constitution. The Eighth Amendment provides: "Excessive bail shall not be required, nor excessive fines imposed, nor cruel and unusual punishments inflicted."[30] James Ingraham was slow to respond to his teacher's instructions. For this, he was hit twenty times with a paddle while he was held over a table in the principal's office. The beating caused a blood clot. He could not attend school for several days. Roosevelt Andrews was paddled on several occasions. On one occasion, he lost the use of his arm for a week. The general rule in states that allowed corporal punishment was that a teacher could use reasonable force to control, train, or educate a child. If the force was excessive or unreasonable, the teacher could be held liable for money damages or be subject to criminal prosecution.

James Ingraham's and Roosevelt Andrews's attorneys acknowledged that the original purpose of the Eighth Amendment was to limit criminal punishments. They argued to the Court, however, that the Eighth Amendment should be extended to the paddling of schoolchildren. If the Eighth Amendment did not apply to schoolchildren, then schoolchildren could be beaten without any constitutional remedy. Was this really fair, given the fact that hardened criminals in prison would have a remedy? Supreme Court Justice Powell delivered the opinion for the Court. The Court found that the Eighth Amendment did *not* apply to the paddling of schoolchildren. Justice Powell wrote that "[t]he prisoner and the schoolchild stand in wholly different circumstances, separated by the harsh facts of criminal conviction and incarceration."[31] According to Justice Powell and the majority of the Court, "[t]he schoolchild has little need for the protection of the

Eighth Amendment." Other legal remedies such as money damages or criminal prosecution of teachers safeguard the children from receiving excessive punishment.[32]

How would the Supreme Court view a request by T.L.O. to apply the Fourth Amendment to public school officials? Would the Fourth Amendment carry the same weight that the First Amendment had in *Barnette* and *Tinker* and the Fourteenth Amendment had in *Goss*? Or would the Court conclude that the rights afforded by the Fourth Amendment did not apply to schoolchildren, as it had about the Eighth Amendment in Ingraham? If the Fourth Amendment did apply, what justification for a search of student property would be necessary—probable cause or reasonable suspicion? Finally, if the search violated the Fourth Amendment, would the evidence seized be admissible at a criminal trial against a student defendant? It was time for the state of New Jersey to seek answers.

3

An Overview of the Case for New Jersey

Kenneth J. Lebrato was an assistant prosecutor in Middlesex County, New Jersey, in 1980. He had just graduated from law school at Gonzaga University in Spokane, Washington, the year before. As a prosecutor Lebrato was responsible for enforcing New Jersey's criminal laws in his county. He was assigned to represent the state of New Jersey against T.L.O. Interestingly, Lebrato had sat on the board of education when he was eighteen years old. He was the youngest elected official in New Jersey at the time.[1]

When Lebrato first received the *T.L.O.* file, his supervisor did not think New Jersey had a very good case. Because of Lebrato's personal interest in schools, he decided to research the issues further. He told his supervisor he thought it was a good case. He recommended that the prosecutor's office proceed against T.L.O.

Juvenile Court Proceedings

Because T.L.O. was a juvenile, the prosecutor's office brought the case against her in the juvenile court. The proceedings in juvenile courts differ greatly from those in adult criminal courts. The idea behind juvenile court is that children are to be treated differently from adults. The goals of the juvenile justice system are to provide guidance and rehabilitation for a child who has committed a crime, and to protect the public. It is not the goal of the juvenile court to punish a child.[2]

In many states the procedures for dealing with juvenile offenders are very informal. Sometimes juvenile offenders will merely receive a warning from a police officer. In other minor cases, the juveniles may be taken to the police station to discuss their behavior with their parents.

In more serious circumstances a juvenile will be taken into custody and charged by a formal complaint. There is no grand jury in juvenile proceedings. Grand jury investigations are reserved for adult cases. A grand jury is a group of citizens who are summoned together by the government. The group hears the testimony of witnesses and examines evidence in a closed room. It is trying to determine whether an adult suspect should be charged with a particular crime. The grand jurors must decide two things based on the evidence presented to them: (1) Whether there is probable cause to believe that a crime has been committed. (2) Whether it is more likely than not that the adult suspect is the person who committed the crime. If it decides the adult suspect should be prosecuted, the grand jury will formally charge the suspect in a document called an indictment. In a juvenile case, the prosecutor alone decides whether to charge the juvenile.

As in adult court, the juvenile will be given the opportunity to either plead guilty to the offense or go to trial. If the juvenile pleads guilty, the judge will issue a sentence and the case will be closed. Some sentences may include removing the juvenile from home and placing him or her in a facility that focuses on drug abuse, repeat offenders, or job training.

Unlike adults who are charged with a crime, juveniles do not have a right to trial by jury. In many states juveniles are also not entitled to use the insanity defense. If the judge determines that a juvenile is a danger to himself or others, the juvenile can also be detained without bail in a juvenile facility. Bail is money deposited with the court by the juvenile's family, or an interested party, to get the juvenile released temporarily. The money serves as an assurance that the juvenile will appear in court for trial or other proceedings.

Unlike those in adult courts, the proceedings in juvenile court are confidential and closed to the public. This is done to protect the juveniles. Juveniles are entitled to remain anonymous. Only attorneys, authorized court employees, and family of the juveniles are allowed to attend juvenile court proceedings.

Also unlike those in adult cases, juvenile case records are confidential. Only those people who are authorized by the court can see the records. Those people usually include defense counsel, the prosecutor, court employees, and the juvenile's family. If others wish to see the records, they must apply for a court order allowing them to do so.

If an adult is charged with a criminal law violation and is found guilty, that person is convicted. If a juvenile is brought before a juvenile court and the judge finds that the accused violated the law, it means that the offender has been judged to be delinquent. In some serious cases, depending on state or federal law, a juvenile can be charged as an adult in an adult criminal court. Those cases usually involve allegations of murder, rape, armed robbery, or other serious crimes. How would T.L.O.'s case proceed through the court system?

Two Motions Filed by T.L.O.'s Lawyer

T.L.O. was charged in juvenile court with possession of marijuana with intent to distribute. She did not plead guilty. She decided to go to trial to fight the charge. As in adult trial courts, attorneys representing juveniles may file motions with the court, asking the court for certain legal rulings. T.L.O.'s lawyer, Frederick A. Simon, filed two motions—a motion to dismiss the complaint and a motion to suppress the evidence. He argued that Assistant Vice Principal Choplick violated T.L.O.'s Fourth Amendment right to privacy when he searched T.L.O.'s purse. Therefore, the evidence seized from the purse should not be used against T.L.O. at trial.

Motions Denied

Assistant Prosecutor Lebrato won a key legal victory early on. Juvenile court Judge George J. Nicola denied both motions. It would be the first significant ruling in a long process of appeals all the way to the United States Supreme Court.

Judge Nicola's written opinion discussed four

theories. These were all being used at the time by courts around the country to deal with searches of student property by public school officials.

1. Some courts had ruled that the Fourth Amendment did not apply to school officials because they act *in loco parentis* (in the place of the parents).[3]

2. Some had ruled that the Fourth Amendment applied but that the exclusionary rule did not. Even if the search violated the student's Fourth Amendment rights, any evidence found could still be used against the student at a trial.[4]

3. Some held that the Fourth Amendment applied but that the school official needed only reasonable suspicion to search. They did not need probable cause.[5]

4. Finally, at least two courts had held that the Fourth Amendment applied *and* probable cause was required in order to search.[6]

Reasonable Suspicion vs. Probable Cause

New Jersey courts fell into the third category—the Fourth Amendment applied but the school official needed only reasonable suspicion of a school violation or of a crime to search. Judge Nicola cited a similar approach used in *In re L. L.* This was a Wisconsin case

Jersey justices rule for 2 students, cite need for 'reasonable' searches

By ROBERT G. SEIDENSTEIN

The state Supreme Court yesterday invalidated two drug-related student searches but said that school officials, under certain circumstances, have the right to go through the property of pupils.

The part of the 5-2 decision invalidating the searches prompted a strong dissent by Justice Sidney Schreiber who accused his colleagues in the majority of undercutting the fight against the "overwhelming problem" of drugs in the public schools.

Schreiber, who was joined in his dissent by Justice Marie Garibaldi, said that in invalidating the searches the majority only paid "lip service to the principle that school officials have the authority to conduct reasonable searches necessary to maintain safety, order and discipline within the sch᠁

the majority, said school administrators have the power to search a student's property when such an action is "reasonable," but added that the officials overstepped their bounds in the two cases—consolidated on appeal—that had been brought before the court.

"Young people and students are persons protected by the United States and New Jersey Constitutions" from unreasonable searches, O'Hern said.

One of the cases decided yesterday ᠁ High School and ᠁nt's purse. ᠁High᠁

The New Jersey Supreme Court ruled in favor of students' rights and against the search of T.L.O.'s purse.

decided shortly before T.L.O.'s motion came before him.[7]

In the case of *In re L. L.*, the Wisconsin court balanced the state's strong interest in educating juveniles in an orderly atmosphere—free from danger and corruption with students' reasonable expectation of privacy in their personal property while in school. The Wisconsin court held that students have a lower expectation of privacy in school, as opposed to outside school. It was expected that schools would restrain students to some degree for security or discipline measures.

Judge Nicola agreed that the Fourth Amendment applied to the search Choplick conducted. However, Choplick needed only reasonable suspicion, not probable cause. According to Judge Nicola, Choplick was justified in opening T.L.O.'s purse. This was because a teacher had seen her smoking in an area where smoking was not permitted. Once inside the purse, and after finding the cigarettes, Choplick ordinarily would not have been justified in searching further. But in this case the marijuana and pipe were in plain view. The plain view doctrine is another exception to the warrant requirement. Under this doctrine, a law enforcement officer can seize any evidence that is in plain sight, if the officer had a right to be in the position to see it.

Judge Nicola ruled that Choplick had a right to seize the drug evidence from T.L.O.'s purse. He had a right to open the purse and take out the cigarettes. Once he did that, he plainly saw the marijuana and pipe. That allowed him to search even further. Judge Nicola denied T.L.O.'s motion to suppress the evidence. Prosecutor Lebrato was permitted to use the evidence at T.L.O.'s trial.

T.L.O. Judged Delinquent

Records of juvenile court proceedings are not open to the public. Because of this, the exact testimony from T.L.O.'s trial is not available. What is known, however, is that Lebrato won another victory on March 23, 1981. After the court heard and saw the evidence, it decided that T.L.O. had committed the crime charged. This meant that T.L.O. had been judged to be delinquent.

To a Higher Court

T.L.O. appealed Judge Nicola's decision to the next higher court, the appellate division of the Superior Court of New Jersey. At that point Lebrato decided to hand the case over to the attorney general for the state of New Jersey. He could have handled the appeal himself, but he had only recently graduated from law school. He felt that the attorney general's office would do a better job.[8]

Middlesex County assistant prosecutor Kenneth J. Lebrato was assigned to represent the state of New Jersey in its case against T.L.O. He initially won his case because T.L.O. was judged to be delinquent by the juvenile court.

The attorney general at the time of T.L.O.'s case was Irwin I. Kimmelman. He was the prosecutor for the entire state. The attorney general has a staff of deputy attorneys general. They handle a variety of civil and criminal cases on behalf of the state. Deputy Attorney General Victoria Curtis Bramson was assigned to represent the state of New Jersey in the T.L.O. appeal.

In a very short written opinion rendered on June 30, 1982, the appellate division upheld the juvenile court's denial of T.L.O.'s motion to suppress evidence.[9] Like the Supreme Court, appellate courts follow the principle of majority rule. In this case, two of the three judges ruled in favor of the state of New Jersey. A third, Judge Charles S. Joelson, did not agree with his colleagues and wrote a separate, dissenting opinion.

Judge Joelson also pointed out that mere possession of cigarettes did not violate any school rule at Piscataway High. The regulations prohibited smoking only in certain areas of the school. Judge Joelson reasoned that because possession of cigarettes was not a violation, the purpose for Mr. Choplick's search was only to catch T.L.O. in a lie. After all, she had told Choplick she did not smoke. Catching a student in a lie, however, was an unreasonable justification for a search under the Fourth Amendment, according to

Judge Joelson. He characterized the search as "riding rough-shod over the rights of a juvenile in school."[10]

The majority of the appellate division agreed with New Jersey on the Fourth Amendment issue. It disagreed, however, with the trial court's ruling on whether T.L.O. had knowingly waived her constitutional rights (under *Miranda* v. *Arizona*) before giving her confession to the police. Therefore, the appellate division voided the judgment of delinquency. It ordered that the case be returned to trial for further proceedings on that one issue. But T.L.O. wanted to continue her appeal of the Fourth Amendment issue. She chose not to go back to the trial court immediately on the confession issue. Instead, she chose to start the next step to appeal the decision of the appellate division on the Fourth Amendment issue. Her attorney filed the appeal and submitted her arguments to the Supreme Court of New Jersey.

To the New Jersey Supreme Court

The appellate division had ruled in favor of the state on the Fourth Amendment issue. Victoria Bramson's work was not finished, however. She would have to respond to T.L.O.'s arguments on appeal. Would the state's winning streak continue? The state of New Jersey, through Bramson, continued to take the position that the Fourth Amendment did not apply to public school officials. The Supreme Court of New Jersey, like all the other courts below it, did not agree. Bramson also argued on behalf of the state of New Jersey that the exclusionary rule (the rule of law that excludes unlawfully seized evidence from a criminal defendant's trial) did not apply where evidence seized by a school official is offered as evidence in a juvenile court proceeding. The Supreme Court of New Jersey rejected that argument too.

Following the reasoning of the lower courts in the state, the Supreme Court of New Jersey first determined that T.L.O. had an expectation of privacy in the contents of her purse. It did not agree with New Jersey that students lose all privacy rights when they enter school. It then determined that a warrantless search of student property by a school official does not violate the Fourth Amendment. As long as the school official "has reasonable grounds to believe that a student possesses evidence of illegal activity or activity that would interfere with school discipline and order," that search is valid.[11] What are reasonable grounds for a search? How would the reviewing courts know whether the school official had reasonable grounds to search?

The New Jersey Supreme Court instructed lower courts in the state to consider certain facts when deciding whether a search was justified. Courts had to consider the child's age and school record. They also had to consider whether the problem prompting the search was serious. In other words, if the child was suspected of hiding drugs in his or her locker, the court should consider whether drugs were a serious problem in the school. The courts also had to consider whether it was necessary to search student property right away. In other words, was there a chance that the student might leave the school with the evidence? The courts also had to consider whether the information provided to school officials and the person providing the information were reliable. The New Jersey Supreme Court warned, however, that as searches become more intrusive—for example, if the school official wants to search clothing the student is wearing—the definition of "reasonableness" will carry a much stricter legal standard.

But here is where the New Jersey Supreme Court parted ways with the lower courts that had reviewed T.L.O.'s case. In the process, it also ended the state's winning streak. In each of the two earlier decisions, the lower courts agreed that because a teacher told Choplick she had seen T.L.O. smoking in the bathroom, Choplick had reasonable suspicion that T.L.O.'s purse would contain evidence of the school violation. Choplick's further search of the purse and discovery of marijuana and evidence of drug dealing was also reasonable, according to the lower courts. The further search was reasonable because he had a right to look inside the purse in the first place.

Search Found Unreasonable in State Supreme Court

The New Jersey Supreme Court, however, sharply disagreed with the lower courts' conclusion that the search was reasonable. The majority of justices followed the dissenting opinion of Judge Joelson from the appellate division in the court below. Justice Daniel O'Hern wrote that mere possession of cigarettes did not violate school rules. Therefore, T.L.O.'s purse did not contain evidence of a violation. Students were permitted to carry cigarettes. Even if T.L.O. had them in her purse, that alone would not have been a school violation. The justices also found that Choplick had no more than "a good hunch" that T.L.O.'s purse contained cigarettes.[12] No one, not even the math teacher, had said she had seen cigarettes in the purse. The Fourth Amendment requires more than a good hunch.

According to the New Jersey Supreme Court, Choplick did not have reasonable suspicion he would find evidence of a school violation or a crime inside

T.L.O.'s purse. Therefore, any evidence he seized from the purse should not have been admitted into evidence at her trial. On August 8, 1983, the Supreme Court of New Jersey reversed T.L.O.'s judgment.

The state of New Jersey had lost its case. It had only one alternative. It could appeal the decision to the court of last resort—the United States Supreme Court. Deputy Attorney General Allan Nodes was chosen for this important task. Interestingly, Allan Nodes and Lois DeJulio, T.L.O.'s new lawyer, had once worked together in the attorney general's office. They were now on opposite sides, though. Nodes had to represent the interests of the state of New Jersey.

The first step Nodes had to take to have New Jersey's case heard by the United States Supreme Court was to file a legal document called a petition for writ of *certiorari*. This is a Latin term that means "to be made certain."[13] A petition for writ of *certiorari* calls "for delivery to a higher court of the record of a proceeding before a lower court."[14] The document generally describes the legal issues that the party, now called the petitioner, wants the higher court to review. The other party, in this case T.L.O., is allowed to file an opposing brief urging the Court not to grant the petition. If the Supreme Court decides that the legal issues in the case require the Court's review, then it will agree to hear the case and grant the petition. The Supreme Court—the highest court in the country—generally selects only those cases that present important federal legal issues that have not yet been decided by the Court. It will also take cases in which there is a conflict among appellate courts around the country about how the issue should be resolved.

Nodes filed a petition for writ of *certiorari* on behalf of the state of New Jersey on October 7, 1983. His petition requested that the Supreme Court decide one issue—whether the exclusionary rule applied to a search of a student by a public school official. The exclusionary rule is a court rule that prohibits the government from admitting into evidence at trial any items seized in violation of the defendant's right against unreasonable searches and seizures. Nodes did not ask the Court to consider the more general issue of whether the Fourth Amendment applied to searches by school officials. New Jersey conceded that the Fourth Amendment applied. However, it wanted the Supreme Court to rule that evidence unlawfully seized by a public school official *is* admissible in a juvenile court case.

To the United States Supreme Court

The United States Supreme Court agreed to hear the case on November 28, 1983. That meant that Nodes would have to prepare a full brief on the issue. T.L.O. would also have an opportunity to respond.

Victoria Bramson was no longer lead counsel in the case. She assisted Nodes, however, in developing the argument raised in the brief. Their central argument was that the exclusionary rule should not be applied to searches of student property by public school officials. According to the state of New Jersey, the most important reason for the exclusionary rule had been to stop illegal searches by law enforcement officers.[15] School officials are not law enforcement officers; they are educators. New Jersey argued that applying the exclusionary rule to their searches would not serve the purpose intended by that rule.

The state also pointed out that school authorities have a duty to maintain a safe environment for their students. In doing so, they need to have broad disciplinary powers. Nodes reminded the Supreme Court about its decision in *Ingraham* v. *Wright*. Here the Court had refused to strike down a school policy allowing school officials to physically punish students.

Friends of the Court Briefs

In some cases before the United States Supreme Court, a person or group other than the original parties will volunteer or be invited by the Court to file a separate brief. This is a way of giving advice to the Court on the pending matter. These groups are known as *amici curiae*, or "friends of the court."[16] In the *T.L.O.* case many other groups offered their advice to the Court. Two groups supported Nodes's argument on behalf of the state of New Jersey.

The New Jersey School Boards Association agreed with New Jersey that the exclusionary rule did not apply. It suggested that the Supreme Court carve out an exception, though. It argued that the exclusionary rule should apply to school searches only if the school official acted in bad faith. It explained this as a situation where the official searches student property, even though he does not have reasonable suspicion to believe that the property contains evidence of a crime or school violation.

The National School Boards Association in Washington, D.C., also presented a brief. It stated its opinion that the Fourth Amendment was not intended to apply to school searches. According to the association, school authorities need to handle disciplinary matters immediately. Rules of criminal law have no place in the school because they are too rigid. The association feared that if the Fourth Amendment applied to schools, teachers and administrators could be subject to search-related lawsuits.

The Washington Legal Foundation also presented a brief. It argued that the exclusionary rule should be restricted to illegal searches conducted by law enforcement officers. After filing their briefs, the state of New Jersey and the school board associations waited for T.L.O.'s response. How would her attorneys address the issues they raised?

4

An Overview of the Case for T.L.O.

In 1980 attorney Frederick A. Simon, a graduate of the University of Kentucky Law School, worked in a New Jersey law firm that handled many types of cases. Through his practice he had come to know T.L.O.'s parents. He had represented them in various legal matters over the years.[1] It was only natural that they called Simon when their daughter was charged with possession of marijuana.

T.L.O.'s Suspension from School

At the time Simon agreed to represent T.L.O., the criminal complaint filed in juvenile court was not T.L.O.'s only headache. Because of the smoking violation and criminal allegations, the board of education had suspended her from school. It suspended T.L.O. for three days for smoking cigarettes and seven days for possession of marijuana. T.L.O.'s parents wanted Simon to appeal the school suspension *and* handle the criminal proceedings. Each proceeding was handled by a different court.

Motion to Set Aside Suspension

Simon filed a motion in a New Jersey civil court asking that the court set aside T.L.O.'s suspensions. Judge David D. Furman heard the matter on March 31, 1980. He did not grant Simon's request to set aside the suspension for T.L.O.'s smoking violation. However, he did agree with Simon's argument that Assistant Vice Principal Choplick had seized evidence from T.L.O.'s purse in violation of her Fourth Amendment rights. Choplick had violated T.L.O.'s rights. Therefore, the evidence he found should not have been used against her at her disciplinary hearing before the school board. Judge Furman set aside T.L.O.'s suspension for possession of marijuana.[2]

Motion to Dismiss Criminal Charges

Armed with Judge Furman's decision from the civil court, Simon filed a motion to dismiss the criminal complaint against T.L.O. in juvenile court. He referred

58

to Judge Furman's opinion. He also argued that because Judge Furman had already ruled on the Fourth Amendment issue, the juvenile court must follow that ruling. The evidence that Choplick found in T.L.O.'s purse should be excluded from the criminal trial.

Simon used two legal doctrines to support this argument. The first doctrine is known as *res judicata*. This is a Latin term meaning "the matter heard and decided by a judge." That rule prevents a party from raising a claim or filing a lawsuit if a court has already made a final decision on that same claim. The second doctrine is called *collateral estoppel*. That doctrine prevents parties from raising a particular issue that has already been decided by a court.

Both Motions Denied

Both of Simon's arguments failed. Juvenile court Judge Nicola ruled that neither legal doctrine applied in this case. Choplick had not violated the Fourth Amendment because he had reasonable suspicion to search T.L.O.'s purse.[3] Having lost this crucial argument, Simon and T.L.O. prepared for trial.

More than one year after the search, during her sophomore year, T.L.O. finally had her day in court. The evidence Choplick seized from T.L.O.'s purse was used against her at her juvenile court hearing. On

59

March 23, 1981, after hearing the testimony of Choplick and others, Judge Nicola found T.L.O. guilty of possession of marijuana with intent to distribute. This finding meant that Judge Nicola had determined T.L.O. to be delinquent.

Judge Nicola did not sentence T.L.O. immediately. The reason was that she was still in the midst of dealing with another charge filed against her in juvenile court—petty larceny. It was not until January 1982, during T.L.O.'s junior year of high school, that she was sentenced to one year probation. As part of her probation, the court ordered her to observe a reasonable curfew, attend school regularly, and successfully complete a counseling and drug therapy program.

T.L.O.'s parents were not interested in appealing the juvenile court's decision. But now that T.L.O. had been judged delinquent by the juvenile court after a trial, the Piscataway Board of Education had more ammunition to punish her further. It began proceedings to expel T.L.O. from Piscataway High School. T.L.O.'s possible expulsion from high school was of great concern to her parents. An expulsion from school meant that T.L.O. would be in violation of her probation. They asked Frederick Simon to continue to represent T.L.O. in her fight against the school board. But they did not have enough money to continue to pay his fee, so they were forced to find another attorney.

In circumstances where a defendant does not have the funds to pay an attorney, there are several alternatives. Some attorneys handle cases for free, or *pro bono.* Other attorneys will agree to handle a case for a smaller fee. This is paid to the attorney directly by the court system. For criminal cases, most states also have public defenders—attorneys who work for a county or state office that handles criminal cases for free to the public. They are paid by the government.

Public Defender Assigned to T.L.O.

T.L.O.'s parents asked the court to appoint a public defender to pick up where Simon had left off. Lois DeJulio was an attorney with the Middlesex County Public Defender Service who had been practicing law for nine years. She was assigned to handle the case. There were still two problems, though. As a criminal defense lawyer, DeJulio was not permitted to handle the expulsion proceedings—they were civil proceedings. She had to figure out another way to stop T.L.O. from being expelled.

T.L.O.'s parents were not really interested in appealing the juvenile court's finding. DeJulio realized, however, that the board of education would not change

Middlesex County Public Defender Lois DeJulio was assigned to handle T.L.O.'s case as it began the appeals process following T.L.O.'s conviction in juvenile court.

its mind about expelling T.L.O. as long as Judge Nicola's ruling of guilty stood. She decided, therefore, that T.L.O. should appeal Judge Nicola's decision.[4] If the appellate division overturned Judge Nicola's ruling, the board of education might not expel T.L.O.

T.L.O.'s second problem was that an appeal of the juvenile court decision would take time. It was not likely that the board of education would wait to expel her until the appeal was decided. Therefore, DeJulio asked the appellate judges to stay, or halt, Judge Nicola's judgment from taking effect until the appeal was decided. The appellate division agreed. The stay meant that T.L.O. had to complete her probation. The actual judgment of delinquency, however, would not be on her record until the end of all court proceedings. The board of education awaited the outcome of T.L.O.'s appeal.

Unfortunately for T.L.O., DeJulio was not successful with her appeal. The majority of the judges (two out of three) upheld Judge Nicola's rulings.[5] But because one judge dissented, T.L.O. had the right to take the case to the next highest court—the New Jersey Supreme Court.

DeJulio argued before the New Jersey Supreme Court that the evidence seized from T.L.O.'s purse should not have been used against her at trial. Choplick had violated T.L.O.'s Fourth Amendment right to privacy by opening the purse. DeJulio argued that Choplick did not have probable cause to believe that T.L.O.'s purse contained cigarettes. The New Jersey Supreme Court ruled that school officials need only reasonable suspicion (not probable cause) of criminal activity or a school violation before conducting a less intrusive search. It also found that Choplick did not have reasonable suspicion. Therefore, the evidence he seized should not have been used against T.L.O. at her trial. The New Jersey Supreme Court reversed Judge Nicola's conviction of delinquency.[6]

The New Jersey Supreme Court decision was a double victory for T.L.O. The court rendered its decision on August 8, 1983—almost two months after T.L.O. graduated from Piscataway High School. That meant that T.L.O. would not have an expulsion on her school record. The court proceedings had lasted beyond her graduation from school.

New Jersey's Appeal to U.S. Supreme Court

One of T.L.O.'s victories was short-lived, however. The board of education could no longer expel her, but the case did not end. The state of New Jersey decided to appeal the decision to the United States Supreme Court. DeJulio had previously worked for the attorney general's office before she became a public defender.

Now she would be up against her former colleague, Deputy Attorney General Allan J. Nodes.

Nodes's brief had addressed only the issue of whether the exclusionary rule applied to searches conducted by public school officials. DeJulio, however, presented a much broader argument to the Supreme Court of the United States. She argued that the Fourth Amendment applies to searches by public school officials because public school officials are employed by the state. They act with authority from the state, and they are responsible for carrying out state laws and regulations.

She then argued that the exclusionary rule should apply in cases where the public school official violates a student's Fourth Amendment rights. According to DeJulio, educators would think twice about conducting unreasonable searches if they knew that any evidence they seized would not be admissible in a criminal trial. She also argued that police officers would not encourage educators to conduct illegal searches. They, too, would realize that any evidence seized could not be used against the defendant in a court of law.

The state of New Jersey was not the only party that had the support of other organizations. The American Civil Liberties Union (national office) and the American Civil Liberties Union of New Jersey, acting as *amici curiae* (friends of the court), filed a brief supporting T.L.O.'s position. They, too, believed that the Fourth Amendment applied to school searches. The exclusionary rule prevented the use of evidence illegally seized by a school official.

Once all the Justices of the Court had read all the briefs filed in the case, the United States Supreme Court scheduled oral arguments for March 28, 1984. It had been a rocky road for T.L.O.'s case and student rights to this point. An unusual twist in the proceedings before the United States Supreme Court would not make the road any smoother.

5

The United States Supreme Court Decides

Lois DeJulio felt very well prepared to present her argument to the United States Supreme Court Justices on the morning of March 28, 1984. She had considerable practice as an appellate attorney in presenting arguments before the New Jersey Supreme Court. Standing before the highest court in the country was a natural progression.[1]

T.L.O. and her family chose not to attend the session. T.L.O. had already graduated from high school. She had also completed her probation successfully. She wanted to avoid more media coverage. At 11:45 A.M., Allan Nodes stood before the United States Supreme Court to begin his oral argument.

Since the very first session of the Supreme Court in 1790, it has been customary for the Chief Justice to sit at the center of the bench. The other eight Justices sit on either side in order of their seniority with the Court. On March 28, 1984, Chief Justice Warren E. Burger was surrounded by Justices William J. Brennan, Byron R. White, Lewis F. Powell, William H. Rehnquist, Thurgood Marshall, Harry A. Blackmun, John Paul Stevens, and Sandra Day O'Connor. Who were these nine Justices? How would their views affect the outcome of the case?

Chief Justice Burger led the conservative wing of the Court. This also included Justices Rehnquist and O'Connor, who usually favored the views of police officers, prosecutors, and trial judges. Burger did not ordinarily vote to extend rights to criminal defendants. Liberal Justices Brennan and Marshall, on the other hand, strongly supported civil liberties. They often questioned the Court's majority position on search and seizure law. Justice Blackmun began his career on the Court by supporting law enforcement. He later began to side with Justices Brennan and Marshall.

The United States Supreme Court begins a new term each year on the first Monday in October. Often the cases it hears reflect political and social controversies of the time. During the 1983–1984 term, when the

Warren Burger was Chief Justice when the Supreme Court heard the case of *New Jersey* v. *T.L.O.*

Supreme Court heard T.L.O.'s case, Ronald Reagan was president of the United States.

During the early 1980s, as in earlier times, the country was involved in a variety of legal battles. African-American fire fighters were protected by an affirmative action program. It required the city of Memphis, Tennessee, to hire a certain number of African Americans as a way of making up for past discrimination. The fire fighters were challenging a plan to lay off workers according to seniority. The layoff would reduce the number of African-American workers. Radio and educational television stations were worried about a federal law that prevented them from voicing their opinions. A national "men only" organization known as the Jaycees had threatened to close two state chapters of their organization because they admitted women.

On the criminal law front, the state of Massachusetts was challenging a decision by its own supreme court. It had reversed a defendant's murder conviction because of technical errors in a search warrant police had used. The state of Iowa was also challenging the reversal of a murder conviction. In that case, police had unlawfully obtained a confession from the defendant. It was inevitable, however, that private citizens would (and did) discover enough evidence to convict him.

Consequently, by the beginning of the 1983–1984 term, a number of cases had made their way to the Supreme Court. The same nine Justices who heard T.L.O.'s case were called upon to decide those cases.

Arguments Begin

Despite its full agenda, on March 28, 1984, the Court turned its attention to the issue presented in *New Jersey v. T.L.O.* Allan Nodes began his argument by telling the Court that New Jersey did not contest the ruling by the New Jersey Supreme Court. The Fourth Amendment does apply to searches of student property by public school officials. One Justice questioned whether "it is open to us to deal with the reasonableness of the search."[2] Again Nodes emphasized that it was not the state's intention to raise that issue. New Jersey agreed with its state Supreme Court's ruling. A school official *should* have reasonable suspicion of criminal activity before a search is conducted. He explained again that New Jersey's quarrel with the state court decision involved *only* the exclusionary rule.

New Jersey's position was that evidence should be admitted at a criminal trial even if the public school official did not have reasonable suspicion of criminal activity or a violation before searching the student's property. In other words, "regardless of how flagrant" a violation of the Fourth Amendment by a public school official, that conduct should not result in exclusion of evidence at trial.[3]

Nodes explained to the Justices that the purpose of the exclusionary rule is to punish law enforcement officers for illegal conduct. Teachers and law enforcement officers have different duties. (Teachers educate and police enforce the law.) Therefore, teachers do not have the same interest in seeing that a defendant is convicted of a crime. According to Nodes, use of the exclusionary rule would not necessarily deter, or prevent, teachers from conducting illegal searches. He also pointed out that there were other ways to deal with a teacher who violates a student's rights. The board of education could fire the teacher.

Lois DeJulio spoke next. The Justices wanted to know which standard she believed should be used to justify a search by school officials. DeJulio had argued before the New Jersey Supreme Court that the stricter standard, probable cause, should be required for a full search. For a less intrusive search, like a frisk of outer clothing for a weapon, she believed the standard should be reasonable suspicion. She told the Justices, however, that the issue of which standard should be used was not before the Court. The state of New Jersey did not raise that issue in its brief. She asked the United States

Supreme Court to accept the decision of the New Jersey Supreme Court. The proper standard in this case was reasonable suspicion. In addition, the exclusionary rule applied because Choplick's search violated T.L.O.'s right to privacy.

Justices Request Additional Information

Having heard the arguments of both attorneys, the Justices of the United States Supreme Court retired to their chambers. They would decide the fate of T.L.O. and the state of New Jersey. In most cases they would have rendered a decision based on the briefs and arguments. But something was not quite right. In an unusual twist, on July 5, 1984, the Supreme Court Justices ordered each attorney to file a supplemental, or additional brief specifically on the issue New Jersey had *not* raised—"Did the assistant principal violate the Fourth Amendment in opening [T.L.O.'s] purse . . . ?"[4]

Why would the Court ask for further briefs and a second oral argument? Yale Kamisar, of the University of Michigan Law School, speculated that the Supreme Court wanted to avoid deciding whether the exclusionary rule applied in T.L.O.'s case.[5] Kamisar felt that because the search was not a random search, and was not outrageous, the Court might find it was reasonable under the Constitution.[6]

Related Opinions Handed Down

On July 5, 1984, the same day that it ordered supplemental briefs in T.L.O.'s case, the Supreme Court handed down opinions in two other cases it had been considering during its 1983–1984 term. Both cases involved searches by police officers. In *United States* v. *Leon*, Justice Byron White wrote that as long as police officers acted in good faith, evidence of a crime would be admitted at a defendant's trial. This would occur even if there were technical errors in the search warrant that the police had used.[7] This is known as the "good faith exception" to the Fourth Amendment's warrant requirement. The Supreme Court also used this "good-faith exception" to uphold a conviction in *Massachusetts* v. *Sheppard*. Here, police had used a defective warrant to find evidence.[8]

Earlier, in June 1984, Chief Justice Warren E. Burger, a staunch supporter of the exclusionary rule, wrote the majority opinion in another case. This case seemed to lessen the rights of those accused of a crime. In *Nix* v. *Williams* the defendant was convicted of first-degree murder in the death of ten-year-old Pamela Powers.[9] Police violated Williams's Sixth Amendment right to counsel. They persuaded him to tell them where he had left the body before a lawyer was present. Chief Justice Burger wrote that evidence of the

Justice Byron White wrote the Supreme Court's opinion in the case of *United States* v. *Leon.* The decision stated that as long as police officers acted in good faith, technical errors in the search process could not exclude evidence found against a defendant.

condition of the body and articles of the child's clothing were properly admitted at trial. The police located the body, however, based on statements they unlawfully obtained from Williams. The Court ruled that evidence is admissible at trial if it would inevitably have been discovered—even if no constitutional violation of the defendant's rights had occurred. This is known as the "inevitable discovery" doctrine. In the *Williams* case, a search party of two hundred persons had already been looking for the child's body. It would inevitably have discovered it on its own.[10]

The cases decided by the Supreme Court during that term dealt with adult defendants outside a school setting. How would these recent decisions affect the arguments raised by the parties in T.L.O.'s case?

Additional Briefs Presented

Nodes's supplemental brief supported the state of New Jersey's original position—that the Fourth Amendment does not apply to school searches conducted by public school officials. The reason it did not apply, Nodes argued, was that T.L.O. had no legitimate expectation of privacy in the contents of her purse in a school environment. He added, however, that even if the Fourth Amendment did apply, Choplick's search of T.L.O.'s purse did not violate her Fourth Amendment rights. He had a reasonable suspicion that the purse contained evidence that she violated a school smoking regulation.

As in her previous briefs, Lois DeJulio's supplemental brief stated that the Fourth Amendment *did* apply to searches by public school officials. Private citizens (including parents) are not subject to the Fourth Amendment. Public school officials, however, are employed by the state and are agents of the government. In this brief, DeJulio did not argue that school officials must have probable cause to search student property. She accepted the New Jersey Supreme Court's ruling. Searches do not violate the Fourth Amendment if the school official had reasonable grounds to believe the student had violated a school regulation or law. She also accepted the lower court's ruling that as the search becomes more intrusive, the definition of reasonable becomes more like the definition of probable cause.

Many organizations again filed briefs as *amici curiae* (friends of the court). Several organizations, such as the National Association of Secondary School Principals and the National School Boards Association, agreed with the state of New Jersey's position. The New Jersey School Boards Association, the National Education Association, and the American Civil Liberties Union supported T.L.O.'s position.

The Fourth Amendment issue had become so hotly contested that even the United States government decided to file an *amicus* brief. The federal government agreed with the New Jersey Supreme Court's ruling. The Fourth Amendment *did* apply to school searches. In addition, reasonable suspicion was sufficient to justify a search by a public school official.

What did attorneys around the country think of this issue? An American Bar Association poll found that 54 percent "probably would agree with the New Jersey Supreme Court's ruling in *T.L.O.* that the search of [T.L.O.'s] purse violated the Fourth Amendment."[11] Female attorneys were more sympathetic to students' rights than male attorneys were. Almost 75 percent of all of the attorneys polled thought that students have a reasonable expectation of privacy in their lockers.[12]

How would the Supreme Court decision affect T.L.O and Assistant Vice Principal Choplick? According to an article in the *American Bar Association Journal*, T.L.O. had already graduated from Piscataway High School. However, she was having difficulty finding a job. The article also stated that Choplick "was relieved of his administrative responsibilities during the same year the [T.L.O.] search occurred. Two years later Choplick lost his teaching job during budget cutbacks."[13] Choplick believed that he lost his teaching job because of the case.[14] "Ironically," the article noted, "Choplick, whose search of a purse sparked the case, now works in a family-run ladies' handbag business in Flemington, N.J."[15]

Second Oral Argument Scheduled

Having read the supplemental briefs of the parties involved and *amici*, the United States Supreme Court scheduled a second oral argument at the beginning of its October 1984 term. Nodes and DeJulio walked into the most prestigious court in the country for the second time on the morning of October 2, 1984.

Nodes was again the first to speak. As expected, he told the Court that the state of New Jersey's position was that neither the Fourth Amendment nor the exclusionary rule applied to school searches. According to Nodes, school officials act *in loco parentis* (in the place of the parent). Because parents are private citizens, they are not subject to Fourth Amendment restrictions. Neither should public school officials be. If, however, a police officer was present during the search, the officer would need probable cause to search without a warrant. He also said that *if* the Fourth Amendment applied, then the standard set by the New Jersey Supreme Court—reasonable suspicion—was the better standard.

The empty interior of the Supreme Court is shown here. This is the same place where the nine Justices of the Supreme Court would sit before the attorneys and spectators, as they listened to arguments in *New Jersey v. T.L.O.*

New Jersey still believed, however, that Vice Principal Choplick had probable cause to search T.L.O.'s purse.

The Justices wanted to know more. Did a school official need reasonable suspicion of a crime before searching student property, or would a violation of a school regulation suffice? Either would suffice, Nodes said. How thorough a search could the official conduct? A pat-down search, a search of a student's jacket, locker, or purse, and possibly even a strip search were reasonable, said Nodes. "Do you think a male teacher could conduct a pat-down search of a young woman student at age sixteen to find the cigarettes?" Justice O'Connor asked.[16] "I believe that that would be constitutionally permissible," responded Nodes.[17] Not even a strip search would be unreasonable, Nodes offered, because "[i]t would not be unreasonable for a private person, and in this instance it is not unreasonable for the state."[18]

Justice Stevens asked if schools could install two-way mirrors in rest rooms. "Yes, they could," said Nodes.[19] "You don't think there is any expectation of privacy in a [rest room]?" asked Justice Rehnquist.[20] The audience laughed. But Nodes replied that two-way mirrors would be allowed if they were placed in the area where "you normally stand to comb your hair. . . ."[21]

The Justices also pressed DeJulio when it was her

turn to speak on behalf of T.L.O. Did the Fourth
Amendment apply in private as well as in public
schools? "[T]he Fourth Amendment has never been
applied to purely private action," DeJulio responded.[22]
Chief Justice Burger suggested that if different rules
apply for public and for private schools, parents might
choose private school for their children. If a student is
caught smoking marijuana, does that give the school
official cause to search her purse? "I think not," DeJulio
responded, "simply because the information did not
implicate that the marijuana was [in her clothing or
purse]."[23] What if the child was chewing gum or using
a crib sheet (to cheat on a test)? According to DeJulio,
chewing gum was not serious enough to warrant a
search. Possession of a cheat sheet might be, however.

What about strip searches? "The search cannot be
reasonable unless there is probable cause at a
minimum," DeJulio responded.[24] What should the test
for reasonableness be? "[A]s the intrusion becomes
more severe, we are talking about probable cause at the
ultimate end," said DeJulio.[25] Can school officials
search a student or that student's property if they saw
the student with a knife instead of cigarettes? "Certainly
when weapons are involved," DeJulio responded.[26] Are
metal detectors permitted in schools? According to
DeJulio, metal detectors violate the Fourth Amendment.

A student is required by the state to be in school and does not voluntarily walk through them.

T.L.O.'s Conviction Upheld

After one hour of probing questions, Nodes and DeJulio had brought to a close their last chances to persuade the Court to rule in their favor. More than three months later, T.L.O. learned that the United States Supreme Court had reversed the decision of the New Jersey State Supreme Court. Her conviction in the trial court was upheld. Her conviction as a delinquent would remain on her record.

How did the Supreme Court arrive at that decision? Did all of the Justices agree? What did the Court's decision mean for the rest of the country? Chief Justice Burger assigned Justice White to write the opinion for the Court. Justice White was the ninety-fourth Justice appointed to the Court. He was appointed by President John F. Kennedy. White's voting record ranged from liberal to conservative on a number of issues.

The Fourth Amendment Judged to Apply to School Searches

The majority of Justices, including Chief Justice Burger and Justices White, Powell, Rehnquist, and O'Connor, had first agreed that the Fourth Amendment applied to searches and seizures conducted by public school

Justice Sandra Day O'Connor was among those in the majority who agreed that the Fourth Amendment did apply to searches and seizures performed by public school officials. In the specific case of *T.L.O.*, the Court ruled that the school's search was reasonable, and should be upheld.

officials. The Justices then agreed that Mr. Choplick's search of T.L.O.'s purse was reasonable. It did not violate the Fourth Amendment. Because the search was justified, the Court declined to state whether or not the exclusionary rule is the proper remedy if a public school official violates the Fourth Amendment.

The Court had reached its first conclusion—that the Fourth Amendment applied to searches and seizures conducted by public school officials. It did this by reviewing the history of the Fourth Amendment. The majority of the Justices did not agree with New Jersey's argument that the Fourth Amendment was intended to regulate only those searches and seizures conducted by law enforcement officers. Justice White noted that the Court had held the Fourth Amendment applicable not only to police officers, but also to building inspectors, Occupational Safety and Health Act (OSHA) inspectors, and even fire fighters.[27] Justice White reasoned that an individual's privacy suffers whether the governmental investigation is for criminal violation or for civil violation. Therefore, the Fourth Amendment applies to both.

The majority of Justices also disagreed with the state of New Jersey's *in loco parentis* argument. Nodes had said that the Fourth Amendment does not apply to public school officials because the authority of teachers and school administrators is more like the authority of parents. It is not like that of the government. Justice White found this argument unrealistic and contrary to the United States Supreme Court's other decisions. He noted that the Supreme Court had held school officials subject to the First Amendment in *Tinker* v. *Des Moines Independent Community School District.* They were subject to the Due Process Clause of the Fourteenth Amendment in *Goss* v. *Lopez.* He then wrote:

> In carrying out searches and other disciplinary functions . . . school officials act as representatives of the State, not merely as surrogates for the parents, and they cannot claim the parents' immunity from the strictures of the Fourth Amendment.[28]

What Justifies a School Search?

The United States Supreme Court had found that the Fourth Amendment applied to public school officials. The next step was for the Court to determine what legal standard justifies searches by a public school official. Did the school official need a warrant? Did the school official need probable cause to search? Was some other lesser standard acceptable?

To answer those questions, the Court asked how it could strike a balance "between the schoolchild's legitimate expectations of privacy and the school's equally legitimate need to maintain an environment in which learning can take place."[29] Nodes had argued on behalf of the state of New Jersey that a schoolchild has virtually no legitimate expectation of privacy in personal property he or she carries to school. The Court disagreed. The Court recognized that it is sometimes difficult to maintain discipline in public schools. It could not, however, find any reason to conclude that schoolchildren waive all their rights to privacy merely by bringing personal items into the school.

If schoolchildren had an expectation of privacy, did that mean that public school officials would be required to obtain a warrant before conducting a search of a student's property? The Court said no. The Justices agreed that warrants are "unsuited to the school environment." They would interfere with "swift and informal disciplinary procedures needed in the schools."[30]

Finally, the Court reached the most important part of its decision. If school officials were not required to obtain a warrant, what legal standard would be applied—probable cause or reasonable suspicion? The Court concluded that "the legality of a search of a student should depend simply on the reasonableness, under all the circumstances, of the search."[31] When exactly is a search reasonable? When the type of search and extent of the search are not "unduly intrusive given the age and gender of the student and the nature of the violation."[32] The Court concluded that the reasonableness standard would not unduly burden school officials. It also would not allow overly intrusive invasions of a student's privacy.

Was Search of T.L.O.'s Purse Reasonable?

The only question that remained was whether Mr. Choplick's search of T.L.O.'s purse was reasonable. The Court first determined that Mr. Choplick acted reasonably when he searched T.L.O.'s purse. A teacher had reported seeing T.L.O. smoking in the girls' bathroom. This gave Mr. Choplick reason to believe T.L.O. might have cigarettes in her purse. The Court recognized that T.L.O. might not have had cigarettes in her purse (she could have borrowed one from someone else). Justice White explained, however, that "reasonable suspicion" does not mean "absolute certainty."[33]

DeJulio had argued that after Mr. Choplick removed the cigarettes and found rolling papers inside T.L.O.'s purse, he exceeded the scope of the search by seizing and reading the letters that implicated her in drug dealing. The Supreme Court was not persuaded by this argument. The Court found that Mr. Choplick's discovery of rolling papers gave him a reasonable suspicion that T.L.O. was carrying marijuana in her purse. That suspicion justified a further look. When that further search turned up a pipe, a number of plastic bags, a small quantity of marijuana, and a fairly substantial amount of money, it was not unreasonable for Mr. Choplick to extend his search to the zippered compartment. There he found the index card listing "people who owe me money" as well as two letters. Justice White wrote, "[W]e cannot conclude that the search for marijuana was unreasonable in any respect."[34]

The United States Supreme Court reversed the New Jersey State Supreme Court's judgment. T.L.O.'s conviction for delinquency would stand. Justices Powell and O'Connor agreed with the majority opinion. They also joined in a separate concurring opinion written by Justice Powell. That opinion placed greater emphasis on the duty of school officials and teachers to educate and train young people. Because of those duties, the two Justices felt that students should not be afforded the same constitutional rights as juveniles outside the school setting. Justice Blackmun also agreed with the majority. His reasoning was different, however, so he too wrote a separate opinion. His opinion emphasized the fact that teachers have neither the training nor the experience to make a quick judgment about whether probable cause exists.

Justices uphold searches and limit student rights

By ROBERT COHEN
Star-Ledger Washington Bureau

WASHINGTON—The Supreme Court ruled yesterday that teachers and principals may search students if they reasonably believe that there has been a violation of the law or school rules.

In a 6-3 decision involving a former New Jersey schoolgirl, the court concluded that students in school are protected by the constitutional guarantee against unreasonable searches, but not to the same degree as adults facing searches by police.

The court said a student's legitimate expectation of privacy in school is not ironclad and must be balanced against the need of school officials to maintain order and discipline.

Justice Byron White, writing ... student ...

that the search will turn up evidence that the student has violated or is violating either the law or the rules of the school."

White said the search must be "reasonable under the circumstances" and "not excessively intrusive in light of the age and sex of the student and the nature of the infraction."

The justice said a stricter standard used by police in searches of adults would be too burdensome in the school setting. In adult cases, police must have "probable cause" that an individual has violated or is violating the law in order to conduct a search.

Although maintaining their standard is similar to the one adopted in 1983 by ... New Jersey Supreme ... te tribu...

T.L.O. was reported by a teacher to have been smoking in the restroom in violation of school rules. After she denied the charge, Assistant Vice Principal Theodore Choplick opened her purse and found cigarettes as well as marijuana paraphernalia and evidence she might be selling marijuana.

The teenager was subsequently prosecuted for delinquency, but the charges were thrown out after the New Jersey Supreme Court said the search was unreasonable and illegal.

White, whose decision reinstates the finding of delinquency, said Choplick's decision to search the purse to look for cigarettes was a "common sense" ... Once he saw the marijuana paraphernalia ... suspicion justified further ...

... Justice Warren ...

In a January 1985 decision, the Supreme Court ruled that teachers and principals may search students if they have reason to believe that there has been a violation of a law or a school rule.

Dissenting Opinions

Justices Brennan and Marshall concurred with the majority. The Fourth Amendment does apply to searches conducted by public school officials. The two Justices emphatically disagreed, however, with the majority's use of the "reasonableness" standard in determining whether Mr. Choplick's search was justified. The two dissenting Justices cited a line of cases, beginning with *Terry* v. *Ohio*. These cases had used a "balancing test" only in situations where the search was slightly intrusive. Justices Brennan and Marshall firmly believed that Mr. Choplick's search was a serious intrusion on T.L.O.'s privacy. Therefore, the Fourth Amendment required that Mr. Choplick have probable cause to search.

The two Justices then concluded that Mr. Choplick did not have probable cause. Their view was that once Mr. Choplick found evidence of a smoking violation, the search was complete. He did not have probable cause to "rummage through T.L.O.'s purse."[35] The mere presence of rolling papers was not sufficient to infer that T.L.O. had violated drug laws. Justices Brennan and Marshall dissented from the Court's majority ruling. They found that Mr. Choplick's search violated the Fourth Amendment.

Lastly, Justice Stevens also wrote a separate

Justice Thurgood Marshall was one of two Justices who disagreed with the
majority opinion that the principal's search of T.L.O.'s purse was reasonable.
He felt that once the cigarettes were found, and evidence of a violation of
school rules was discovered, the search should have ended.

dissenting opinion. He had disagreed with the Court's decision to order additional briefs and arguments in this case. The state of New Jersey's initial brief had raised only one issue—whether the New Jersey State Supreme Court had erred when it ruled that the evidence seized from T.L.O.'s purse was not admissible at her trial. In other words, had the search violated the Fourth Amendment? Justice Stevens believed that the "simple and correct answer" in this case was to uphold the judgment of the New Jersey State Supreme Court. The evidence seized from T.L.O.'s purse should not have been admissible in Court. It was not necessary for the Court to decide whether the Fourth Amendment was violated. The state of New Jersey had not even raised that issue. By ordering supplemental briefs and a second oral argument to decide an issue that was not raised, the Supreme Court had raised and decided an issue it thought was important even though the parties involved had not raised that issue in their arguments.[36]

Educators, students, and parents across the state of New Jersey had mixed reactions to the Supreme Court's ruling. Saul Cooperman was commissioner of education. He applauded the decision. He stated in an interview with the *Newark Star Ledger*, "The protection of the school community has got to be the first consideration of any administrator, even if it means giving up some rights of the minority."[37] James Koch, the principal of Piscataway High School, called the decision "fantastic."[38]

Victory Claimed by Both Sides

Both DeJulio and Nodes claimed victory. DeJulio said, "At least now, we have accepted [that] children do have Fourth Amendment protections and at least the Supreme Court didn't totally kiss their privacy goodbye."[39] Nodes said the state of New Jersey was "very happy with the ruling."[40] "You can't just walk up to a student and stick your hand in their pocket. . . . But you can stick your hand in his pocket if you suspect there is contraband, like cigarettes, there."[41]

T.L.O. was nineteen years old by the time the decision came down from the United States Supreme Court. She did not talk to the media. DeJulio said she was "very shy and not at all comfortable with being a test case."[42] Other high school students had mixed opinions. One student was quoted as saying, "It's ridiculous."[43] Other students said they thought that school officials should have proof that a student had violated a school regulation or committed a crime before they could search. Some parents were confused about the ruling. One parent thought the Supreme Court may have gone too far.[44]

The United States Supreme Court emphasized in the *T.L.O.* decision that there were certain issues it would not decide in the case. It had decided that the search in the *T.L.O.* case was lawful. Because of this, it declined to decide whether the exclusionary rule applied to unlawful searches conducted by school officials. It also would not give an opinion on whether a school official could search a student only if the official had reason to suspect that particular student of a crime or a school violation.

The Court also declined to state an opinion about what legal standard would apply if a search was conducted by either a school official or a police officer if both were present. Finally, it would not decide in *T.L.O.* whether students had a legitimate expectation of privacy in school-owned property such as lockers and desks. The Court decided only the specific issues presented to it in the facts of the *T.L.O.* case.

Interestingly, the Court noted that New Jersey could insist on a more demanding legal standard—like probable cause—by drafting a new law or including it in the state constitution. School officials would then be subject to the standard specifically required by New Jersey law.

Remember that the New Jersey Appellate Division had ruled that T.L.O.'s case should be sent back to the trial court. That court was to look solely at the issue of whether her constitutional rights were violated when she confessed to the police. Once the Supreme Court rendered its final decision on the Fourth Amendment issue, T.L.O. could have gone back to the trial court for further proceedings on the confession issue. (The United States Supreme Court had not stated an opinion on that issue.) After her loss in the Supreme Court, however, T.L.O. did not want to continue with any further court proceedings. She accepted the Supreme Court's ruling and the entire case ended.

During the next decade, legal scholars would remark that various Supreme Court decisions, including T.L.O.'s case, were weakening the guarantees of the Fourth Amendment. Would the Supreme Court change its mind about public school searches, or would *New Jersey* v. *T.L.O.* remain good law?

6

The Future of Reasonable Searches

The Supreme Court's decision in *New Jersey* v. *T.L.O.* settled many of the nagging questions that schools around the country had tried to resolve for many decades. It finally carved out the legal standard that public school officials would be required to use before they could search the property of students suspected of committing a crime or violating a school regulation. But as with everything in life, things would change. Many changes would occur in our country and in our school systems over the years following the decision in *New Jersey* v. *T.L.O.* These changes would test the strength of the decision in that case. What were those changes? How would *New Jersey* v. *T.L.O.* hold up?

Lawyers presenting briefs in the *T.L.O.* case had alerted the Supreme Court to some shocking statistics. Included among them was the fact that violence in schools was increasing. According to the brief filed by the National School Boards Association, citing a 1978 study, "Nearly three million school children may be the victims of crime each month."[1] Justice White noted in the 1985 *T.L.O.* decision that "in recent years, school disorder has often taken particularly ugly forms: drug use and violent crime in the schools have become major social problems."[2] In 1985 the only question before the Court, however, was whether, and under what standard, a public school official acting alone could legally search a student's personal property.

During the decade following *T.L.O.*, violence and drug use in the schools increased. School officials struggled with the question of how to protect their students and maintain order on school property. Possession of guns, knives, and drugs by some students threatened the school environment—and other students. How would school officials cope with these changes? Would individual searches by public school officials be adequate to protect students? How would advances in technology change the way searches are conducted? Would the courts uphold these new search methods?

Much in the same way that the Justices of the United States Supreme Court were not unanimous in their decision of the *T.L.O.* case, people in New Jersey had mixed opinions about the decision.

Cases That Followed *T.L.O.*

In the mid-1990s a high school in Philadelphia installed a metal detector to scan student property. As students entered the school, they were led to the gymnasium, where they were required to empty their pockets and hand over their jackets and bags to be searched. Each student was then scanned by the metal detector. One student, with the initials F. B., emptied his pockets and surrendered a Swiss army-type knife. School officials escorted him to a holding room where police charged him with possession of a weapon on school property. F. B. challenged the search in court.

In one of the first reported metal detector cases, the Pennsylvania Superior Court upheld the search as reasonable, even though school officials had no individualized suspicion that F. B. was armed.[3] The court concluded that "the search was justified at its inception because of the high rate of violence in the Philadelphia public schools."[4]

Courts in Illinois and Florida followed the decision in the Pennsylvania case. In Chicago, Fenger High School enlisted the local police department to help conduct metal detector searches at the school.[5] As one student passed through the detector, it registered a positive reading. A police officer patted him down and found a loaded .38 caliber revolver in his pants pocket.

The student challenged the search. He argued that it was invalid because he did not consent to it. The Illinois Appellate Court disagreed. The court followed the reasoning of *New Jersey* v. *T.L.O.* It tried to strike a balance between the student's expectation of privacy and the school's need to maintain a safe learning environment. The court first recognized that "[j]udges cannot ignore what everybody else knows: violence and the threat of violence are present in the public schools. The situation has worsened in the past 11 years. School children are harming each other with regularity."[6] The court then found that the purpose of the metal detector screening was to protect the school for all students. It was not there to investigate a particular crime. All students were required to walk through the detectors and the intrusion was minimal. No student was touched by an officer unless the detector reacted. Once the metal detector reacted, the court held, a frisk was justified.

Florida courts followed this trend in the mid-1990s. The Dade County School Board adopted a policy allowing random searches of students by using metal detector wands. At the time, metal detector searches were routine and constitutional in places like airports and courthouses. In the Dade County schools, the board of education hired an independent security team. It was to conduct random searches in randomly selected areas of each school. The search team was accompanied by a school official. They would enter a classroom and ask the students to empty their pockets. The team would then scan the students with the metal detector wand. If the wand reacted, the security officer would pat down the student or look inside the student's property, such as a purse or book bag. Students were allowed to refuse to be searched. Refusal could subject them to various disciplinary actions, however. If the search team discovered illegal drugs or weapons, the school notified police officers. Students could be arrested as a result of the search.

After this policy came into effect, a student with the initials J. A. was arrested in a Florida public high school. The search team entered J. A.'s classroom. The assistant principal watched as someone passed a jacket to the back of the room. One of the students placed the jacket on a shelf. A security team member took the jacket from the shelf and scanned it. He discovered a gun inside the jacket. The team found out that J. A. owned the jacket.

Citing the Illinois court's decision in *People* v. *Pruitt*, the Florida court upheld the search of J. A.'s jacket. The Florida Appellate Court, too, recognized that violence had escalated in its schools: "The incidences of violence in our schools have reached alarming proportions. In the year prior to the Board's implementation of the search policy, Dade County Public Schools reported both homicides and aggravated batteries as well as the confiscation from students of a very high number of weapons, including handguns."[7] The court balanced the students' privacy, the type of search, and the need for the search. It held that the search of J. A.'s jacket was both reasonable and constitutional.

Violence was not the only problem on the rise in schools. Drug use was also increasing. Challenges to a different form of Fourth Amendment search—random drug testing in public schools—reached the United States Supreme Court in 1995. The decision in *Vernonia School District* v. *Acton* would become another landmark decision.[8] In the mid- to late-1980s teachers and administrators in the Vernonia school district in Oregon noticed a sharp increase in drug use by their students. The district determined that student athletes appeared to be the leaders of the drug culture. School officials were particularly concerned about the increased risk of sports-related injuries due to drug use.

The school board approved a policy that applied to all students who wanted to play sports. Students and their parents were required to sign consent forms. The forms allowed the school to randomly test the students for drug use by taking urine samples. In 1991 a seventh

Since *New Jersey* v. *T.L.O.*, the United States Supreme Court has taken on several more cases concerning how constitutional rights apply to students attending public schools.

grader named James Acton signed up to play football. But the school would not allow him to play because he and his parents refused to sign the testing consent forms. The Actons challenged the school district's policy at every level of the judicial system. Finally, the case reached the United States Supreme Court.

Justice Antonin Scalia wrote the opinion for the majority. The first issue he considered was whether students have a legitimate privacy interest against the kind of search the school wanted to conduct. Justice Scalia explained the difference between private school and public school. In a private school, teachers and school officials stand *in loco parentis* (in place of the parents). In private schools, students do not have the right to come and go at will. The actions of private school teachers and officials, therefore, are not subject to the requirements of the Fourth Amendment.

Justice Scalia wrote that teachers and administrators in *public* schools must comply with the Fourth Amendment. This was the same conclusion the Court had reached in *New Jersey* v. *T.L.O.* Students do have some expectation of privacy, but schools act reasonably when they require physical examinations, vaccinations, and other screenings for problems in vision or hearing. Scalia cited Justice Powell's opinion in *T.L.O.*: "[S]tudents within the school environment have a lesser expectation of privacy than members of the population generally."[9] Justice Scalia wrote in the *Vernonia* decision that school athletes have a "reduced expectation of privacy." They voluntarily subject themselves to preseason physical exams, they must have adequate insurance coverage, and they choose to comply with rigid rules of conduct.

The Supreme Court found that providing a urine sample was very little intrusion, if any, into a student's privacy. The concern of the state, however, was very important. Studies had shown that drugs affect not only the students who use them but the entire student body and faculty. The educational process is disrupted by the physical, psychological, and addictive effects of drug use.

The majority of the Court agreed that student athletes have a lesser expectation of privacy, that urine testing is a minimal intrusion on their privacy, and that the concerns of the state are great. The Supreme Court concluded that random drug testing in this case was reasonable and constitutional.

The future of searches by public school officials is still developing. It appears from the cases decided since *New Jersey* v. *T.L.O.* that the Supreme Court is inclined to allow those types of searches that involve only a slight intrusion on the student's privacy. This is true in cases where the state has a compelling interest in conducting the search. Recent state case law indicates that schools are becoming increasingly more concerned about drugs and violence. Those concerns will justify searches under certain conditions. With the development of more advanced technology, however, how intrusive will searches become? Will metal detectors and drug testing still be constitutional if student drug use is proven to be on the decline? If drug use and violence continue to increase, will courts permit more intrusive searches? The future holds many interesting issues to be considered by schools, students, state courts, and undoubtedly, the United States Supreme Court.

Questions for Discussion

1. You are the vice principal of a public high school. While walking down the hall during a change in classes you see two students fighting. One student appears to have a metal object in her hand. By the time you make your way through the crowd and reach the students, you no longer see the metal object. Do you have reasonable suspicion of criminal activity or a violation of a school regulation to search the student? If you believe you have reasonable suspicion, can you search the student's locker? Can you search her purse? Her jacket? Which of the cases discussed earlier supports your position?

2. Discuss the difference between probable cause and reasonable suspicion. Give examples of when a police officer might have probable cause and when a public school official might have reasonable suspicion to justify a search.

3. You are the principal of a private high school. A school regulation prohibits smoking except in designated areas. The regulation does not prohibit possession of cigarettes, however. You have just seen a student smoking a cigarette in violation of a school regulation. You want to search the student's duffel bag. What do you tell the student when he says that searching his duffel bag would be a violation of his Fourth Amendment right to privacy?

4. The year is 2050. Violence in public schools has increased tremendously. Schools now want to strip-search all students as they enter school in the morning. You are an attorney in the public defender's office. What arguments will you make opposing this new rule? What arguments would you make if you were a prosecutor?

5. In *New Jersey* v. *T.L.O.* the Supreme Court did not decide if the exclusionary rule is a proper remedy for a Fourth Amendment violation in a public school setting. If you were a Supreme Court Justice and had to decide this issue, would you rule that evidence obtained unlawfully by a public school official should not be used against the defendant at a criminal trial? If so, why? If not, why not?

6. Do you agree with the United States Supreme Court decision in *New Jersey* v. *T.L.O.?* Discuss your reasons. Include references to the arguments made by each attorney in the case.

7. The year is 2015. Statistics show that violence in schools has decreased substantially since the 1990s. Your school still uses random metal detector searches to search personal property and clothing for weapons. How would you use recent statistics to challenge these searches? Could you still make the same arguments if statistics showed that drug use had substantially decreased among students?

8. Think about and discuss what new types of technology might be invented to aid searches of student property in the future. Discuss whether you think the new technology will be reasonable and constitutional.

9. You are the governor of the state of New Jersey. Given the Supreme Court's ruling in *New Jersey* v. *T.L.O.* (that school officials need only reasonable suspicion to justify a search of student property), would you favor laws or an amendment to the New Jersey constitution to require school officials to have probable cause? Explain your answer. If so, under what circumstances would officials need probable cause?

Chapter Notes

Chapter 1

1. Transcript of motion to suppress, pp. 14–18, heard before the Juvenile and Domestic Relations Court of Middlesex County, N.J., on September 26, 1980, as included in the Brief for Petitioner to the Supreme Court of the United States, Record No. 83-712 (*New Jersey* v. *T.L.O.*).

2. *Miranda* v. *Arizona*, 384 U.S. 436 (1966).

Chapter 2

1. Samuel Adams, *The Writings of Samuel Adams*, vol. 2 (H. A. Cushing, 1906), pp. 350–369.

2. Ibid.

3. Fourth Amendment to the Constitution of the United States.

4. *Boyd* v. *United States*, 116 U.S. 616 (1886).

5. *Weeks* v. *United States*, 232 U.S. 383 (1914).

6. *Marron* v. *United States*, 275 U.S. 192 (1927).

7. *Carroll* v. *United States*, 267 U.S. 132, (1925).

8. *Terry* v. *Ohio*, 392 U.S. 1 (1968).

9. Ibid., p. 30.

10. *Michigan* v. *Long*, 463 U.S. 1032 (1983).

11. *Boyd* v. *United States*, 116 U.S. 616 (1886).

12. *Wolf* v. *Colorado*, 338 U.S. 25 (1949).

13. Fourteenth Amendment to the Constitution of the United States.

14. *Mapp* v. *Ohio*, 367 U.S. 643 (1961).

15. *D.R.C.* v. *State*, 646 P.2d 252 (Alaska App. 1982); *In re G.*, 11 Cal.App.3d 1193, 90 Cal.Rptr. 361 (1970); *In re Donaldson*, 269 Cal. App. 2d 509, 75 Cal.Rptr. 220 (1969); *R.C.M.* v. *State*, 660 S.W.2d 552 (Tex.App. 1983).

16. Eugene Ehrlich, *Amo, Amas, Amat and More*, 1st ed. (New York: Harper & Row, 1985), p. 154.

17. Brief for the United States as Amicus Curiae Supporting Reversal, p. 18, as included in Record No. 83-712 (*New Jersey* v. *T.L.O.*) of the Supreme Court of the United States (quoting 1 W. Blackstone, *Commentaries*, p. 453).

18. *State* v. *Mora*, 307 So.2d 317 (La.), vacated; 423 U.S. 809 (1975), on remand, 330 So.2d 900 (La. 1976).

19. *Bellnier* v. *Lund*, 438 F.Supp. 47 (NDNY 1977); *State* v. *Baccino*, 282 A.2d 869 (Del.Super. 1971); *State* v. *D.T.W.*, 425 So.2d 1383 (Fla.App. 1983); *In re J.A.*, 85 Ill.App.3d 567 (1980); *People* v. *Ward*, 62 Mich.App. 46 (1975); *Doe* v. *State*, 88 N.M. 347 (1975); *People* v. *D*, 34 N.Y.2d 483 (1974); *State* v. *McKinnon*, 88 Wash.2d 75 (1977); *In re L.L.*, 90 Wis.2d 585 (1979).

20. *Board of Education* v. *Barnette*, 319 U.S. 624 (1943).

21. *Tinker* v. *Des Moines School District*, 393 U.S. 503 (1969).

22. Ibid., p. 511.

23. Ibid., p. 513.

24. Ibid., p. 514.

25. Ibid., p. 522.

26. Ibid., pp. 523–524.

27. Ibid., pp. 525–526.

28. *Goss* v. *Lopez*, 419 U.S. 565 (1975).

29. *Ingraham* v. *Wright*, 430 U.S. 651 (1977).

30. The Eighth Amendment to the Constitution of the United States.

31. *Ingraham* v. *Wright*, 430 U.S. at 669.

32. Ibid., p. 670.

Chapter 3

1. Phone interview with Kenneth Lebrato, January 8, 1997.

2. *Kent* v. *United States*, 383 U.S. 541, 554–555 (1966).

3. *State in Interest of T.L.O.*, 428 A.2d 1327, 1332 (Juvenile and Domestic Relations Court, NJ, 1980).

4. Ibid.

5. Ibid.

6. Ibid., p. 1333.

7. *In re L.L.*, 280 N.W.2d 343 (Wis. App. 1979).

8. Phone interview with Kenneth Lebrato, January 8, 1997.

9. *State in Interest of T.L.O.*, 448 A.2d 493 (NJ 1982).

10. Ibid., p. 495.

11. *State in Interest of T.L.O.*, 463 A.2d 934, 941–942 (NJ 1983).

12. Ibid., p. 942.

13. Eugene Ehrlich, *Amo, Amas, Amat and More*, 1st ed. (New York: Harper & Row, 1985), p. 79.

14. Ibid.

15. Brief for Petitioner, p. 7, as included in Record No. 83-712 (*New Jersey* v. *T.L.O.*) of the Supreme Court of the United States, p. 7.

16. Ehrlich, p. 42.

Chapter 4

1. Phone interview with Frederick A. Simon, December 16, 1996.

2. *T.L.O.* v. *Piscataway Board of Education*, No. C2865-79 (Super.Ct.N.J., Ch. Div., March 31, 1984).

3. *State in Interest of T.L.O.*, 428 A.2d 1327 (Juvenile and Domestic Relations Court, NJ, 1980).

4. Phone interview with Lois DeJulio, December 5, 1996.

5. *State in Interest of T.L.O.*, 448 A.2d 493 (Appellate Division, NJ, 1982).

6. *State in Interest of T.L.O.*, 463 A.2d 934 (NJ 1983).

Chapter 5

1. Phone interview with Lois DeJulio, December 5, 1996.

2. Transcript of March 28, 1994, oral argument before the Supreme Court, p. 7, as included in Record No. 83-712 (*New Jersey* v. *T.L.O.*) of the Supreme Court of the United States.

3. Ibid., p. 13.

4. Supplemental Brief for Petitioner Upon Re-argument, p. 5, as included in Record No. 83-712 (*New Jersey* v. *T.L.O.*) of the Supreme Court of the United States.

5. David O. Stewart, "In the Supreme Court: And in Her Purse the Principal Found Marijuana," *American Bar Association Journal*, February 1985, vol. 71, p. 54 (quoting Yale Kamisar).

6. Ibid.

7. *United States* v. *Leon*, 468 U.S. 897 (1984).

8. *Massachusetts* v. *Sheppard*, 468 U.S. 981 (1984).

9. *Nix* v. *Williams*, 467 U.S. 431 (1984).

10. Michael S. Serrill, "A Matter of Good Faith," *Time*, July 16, 1984, p. 57 (quoting Associate Attorney General D. Lowell Jensen).

11. Lauren Rubenstein Reskin, "In the Supreme Court: Lawyers Support Students' Rights," *American Bar Association Journal*, February 1985, vol. 71, p. 54.

12. Ibid.

13. Stewart, p. 54.

14. Ibid.

15. Ibid.

16. Transcript of October 2, 1984, oral argument before the Supreme Court, p. 13, as included in Record No. 83-712 (*New Jersey* v. *T.L.O.*) of the Supreme Court of the United States.

17. Ibid.

18. Ibid., p. 20.

19. Ibid., p. 26.

20. Ibid., p. 25.

21. Ibid., p. 26.

22. Ibid., p. 32.

23. Ibid., pp. 33–34.

24. Ibid., p. 40.

25. Ibid.

26. Ibid.

27. *New Jersey* v. *T.L.O.* 469 U.S. 325, 335 (1985), citing *Camara* v. *Municipal Court*, 387 U.S. 523 (1967), *Marshall* v. *Barlow's, Inc.* 436 U.S. 307 (1978), and *Michigan* v. *Tyler*, 436 U.S. 499 (1978).

28. *New Jersey* v. *T.L.O.*, 469 U.S. 325, 336–337 (1985).

29. Ibid., p. 340.

30. Ibid.

31. Ibid., p. 341.

32. Ibid., p. 342.

33. Ibid., p. 346.

34. Ibid., p. 347.

35. Ibid., p. 368.

36. Ibid., pp. 374–375.

37. Judy Peet, "Jerseyans Split on The Ruling," *Newark Star Ledger*, January 16, 1985, p. 10.

38. Ibid.

39. Ibid.

40. Ibid.

41. Ibid.

42. Ibid.

43. Ibid.

44. Ibid.

Chapter 6

1. Brief of National School Boards Association, p. 10, Record No. 83-712 (*New Jersey* v. *T.L.O.*) of the Supreme Court of the United States, (citing National Institute of Education, *Violent Schools—Safe Schools: The Safe School Study Report to the Congress*, 1978, pp. 31–32.

2. *New Jersey* v. *T.L.O.*, 469 U.S. 325, 339 (1985).

3. *In the Interest of F. B.*, 658 A.2d 1378 (Pa. Sup. 1995).

4. Ibid., p. 1382.

5. *People* v. *Pruitt*, 662 N.E.2d 540 (Ill.App. 1 Dist. 1996).

6. Ibid., p. 546.

7. *State* v. *J. A.*, 679 So.2d 316, 320 (Fla.App. 3 Dist. 1996).

8. *Vernonia* v. *Acton*, 115 S.Ct. 2386 (1995).

9. *New Jersey* v. *T.L.O.*, 469 U.S. 325, 348 (1985).

Glossary

amicus curiae brief—A brief filed by an individual or organization (such as the ACLU) that is not a party to the case but that has an interest in the outcome of the case. *Amicus curiae* is a Latin term meaning "friend of the court." The plural form of this term is *amici curiae.*

brief—A legal document stating the facts and legal theories of a party's case.

collateral estoppel—The doctrine that prevents parties from raising a particular issue that has already been decided by a court.

dissenting opinion—A written opinion by those Justices who disagree with the majority court opinion.

due process—A legal concept that establishes procedures to insure an individual's rights and liberties in all legal proceedings.

evidence—Information consisting of testimony of witnesses, documents, or tangible objects, that tend to prove the prosecutor's or defense attorney's case. The judge presiding over the trial determines whether the evidence is admissible, whether the jury will be allowed to hear or see the evidence. Evidence can be either direct or circumstantial.

exclusionary rule—A rule of law providing that in certain circumstances unlawfully seized evidence—evidence that is seized in violation of an individual's Fourth Amendment right against unreasonable searches and seizures—is inadmissible in state or federal criminal trials.

good faith exception—A rule of law providing that as long as police officers acted in good faith, evidence of a crime would be admitted at a defendant's trial. This would occur even if there were technical errors in the search warrant that the police had used.

grand jury—A group of citizens summoned by the government to hear the testimony of witnesses and examine evidence in order to determine whether there is probable cause to believe that a crime has been committed and that the suspect is the person who committed the crime.

incorporation doctrine—A legal theory used by the United States Supreme Court to apply the Bill of Rights to the states through the due process clause of the Fourteenth Amendment.

inevitable discovery doctrine—A legal concept providing that unlawfully seized evidence is admissible at trial if the evidence would inevitably have been discovered by lawful means.

in loco parentis—A Latin phrase meaning "in the place of a parent."

motion—A legal document asking the court to rule on a particular legal issue. For example, a motion to suppress evidence is a request for the court to find that evidence seized by police is not admissible at trial because it was seized in violation of the defendant's constitutional rights.

petition for writ of *certiorari*—A legal document that must be filed by any convicted defendant who wants the United States Supreme Court to hear his or her case.

plain view doctrine—An exception to the warrant requirement. Under this doctrine, a law enforcement officer can seize any evidence that is in plain sight, if the officer had a right to be in the position to see it.

prosecutor—An attorney, also known as a district attorney or a United States attorney, who represents the state or federal government in criminal proceedings.

res judicata—This is a Latin term meaning "the matter heard and decided by a judge."

warrant—A legal document authorizing a law enforcement official to take some action. For example, a search warrant authorizes a law enforcement official to search for particular items; an arrest warrant authorizes the arrest of a suspect. In order to obtain a search warrant, a judge or magistrate must find that law enforcement officials applying for the warrant have probable cause to believe the thing or place to be searched contains evidence of a crime. In order to obtain an arrest warrant, a judge or magistrate must find that law enforcement officials applying for the warrant have probable cause to believe that the person to be arrested committed a crime.

Further Reading

Alderman, Ellen, and Kennedy, Caroline. *The Right to Privacy.* New York: Alfred A. Knopf, Inc., 1995.

David, Andrew. *Famous Supreme Court Cases.* Minneapolis, Minn.: Lerner, 1980.

Habenstreit, Barbara. *Changing America and the Supreme Court.* New York: Julian Messner, 1970.

Jenkins, George H. *American Government: The Constitution.* Vero Beach, Fla.: Rourke, 1990.

Lewis, Anthony. *Gideon's Trumpet.* New York: Random House, 1964.

Lowe, William. *Human Rights: Blessings of Liberty: Safeguarding Civil Rights.* Vero Beach, Fla.: Rourke, 1992.

Rehnquist, William H. *The Supreme Court—How It Was, How It Is.* New York: William Morrow, 1987.

Ritchie, Donald A. *Know Your Government: The U.S. Constitution.* New York: Chelsea House, 1989.

Sexton, John, and Nat Brandt. *How Free Are We?: What the Constitution Says We Can and Cannot Do.* New York: M. Evans, 1986.

Index